DAVID ROSS is presently tortured by his love affair with Scotland, something that was not inflicted on him but born with him. He sees cars as handy tools, to take you from A to B, but motorcycles as vibrant, living things. A motorcycle is a man's horse, an extension of his personality, an object not so huge that one cannot find a corner to squeeze into, while you explore a nearby castle or ancient battle site. It's just unfortunate he is burdened with this passion for motorcycling at the same time as being a Scot, since this means that during cold dreich winter days he is often welded to his machine by ice. In spite of this, he still stands 6ft 5ins tall, and is such a fabulous musician that he was once voted best guitarist in his street.

This work is a sequel to *On the Trail of William Wallace* and is as unconventional and unashamedly patriotic as its forerunner. There is nothing wrong with academic history books, it's just that David Ross is not one to sit on the fence. He would rather jump down hard on one side of it, and probably, being a Scot, he would land with a squelch.

On the Trail of Robert the Bruce

DAVID R. ROSS

Luath Press Limited

EDINBURGH

www.luath.co.uk

First Edition 1999

The paper used in this book is acid-free, neutral-sized and recyclable.
It is made from low chlorine pulps produced in a low energy, low
emission manner from renewable forests.

Printed and bound by
Bell & Bain Ltd., Glasgow

Typeset in 10.5 point Sabon by
S. Fairgrieve, Edinburgh, 0131 658 1763

We have been freed from so many and so great evils by the valour of our Lord and Sovereign, Robert Bruce. Like Judas Maccabeus or Joshua, he gladly endured every danger to save his people and kingdom from their enemies

Declaration of Arbroath 1320

Acknowledgements

I would like to thank Karen and Kimberley; Bob McCutcheon, Bookseller of Stirling, for his stories and guidance, and for generously allowing me to reproduce photographs and illustrations from books in his extensive collection, in particular:

Vues Pittoresques de l'Écosse A Pichot (text), F.A. Pernot (engravings), 1827
Pictorial History of Scotland James Taylor, 1859
Border Antiquities of England and Scotland Walter Scott, 1814
Scotland Illustrated Dr William Beattie (text), T. Alcom, W.H. Bartlett and H. McCulloch (illustrations), 1838;

Anthony Fury for his line drawings; Jim Lewis for his maps and battle plans; Catriona Scott, editor; Linda Donnelly for her hard work and willingness to argue with me; Jennie Renton, also for her hard work and willingness to argue with me; Bob the barber for all the haircuts he has given me, man and boy; Hugh Robertson for his swordplay; John Izzett for his wealth of experience; Elspeth King for her continued support; the country of Belgium for its beer; and anyone out there who is not deceived by propaganda.
For one nation to control another is a hateful thing. Pride in ourselves lets us recognise the abilities of others. All people die – not all people really live. Do not fear going forward slowly, fear only to stand still.

Contents

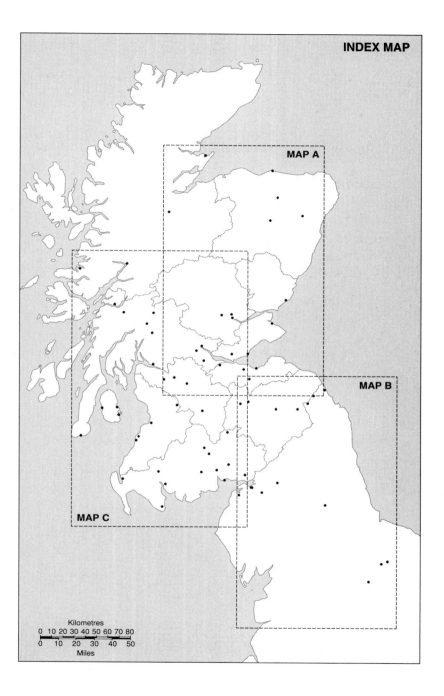

INDEX MAP

MAP A

MAP B

MAP C

Kilometres
0 10 20 30 40 50 60 70 80
0 10 20 30 40 50
Miles

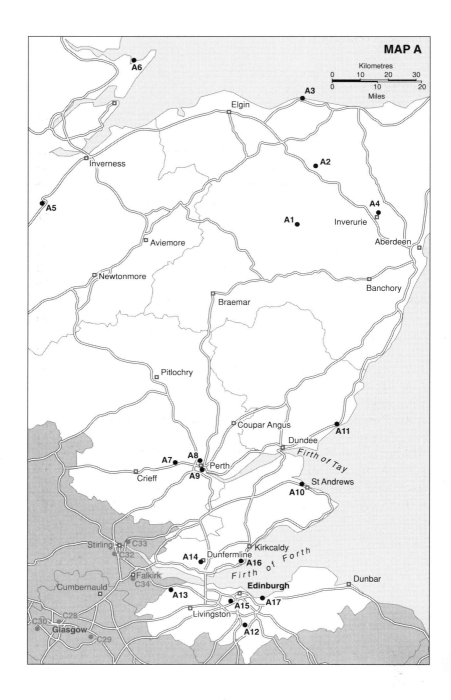

MAP A

Kilometres
0 10 20 30

0 10 20
Miles

A6

A3

Elgin

Inverness

A2

A5

A4

A1

Inverurie

Aberdeen

Aviemore

Newtonmore

Banchory

Braemar

Pitlochry

Coupar Angus

A11

Dundee

Firth of Tay

A7 A8

Perth

Crieff A9

St Andrews

A10

Stirling C33

C32

A14 Dunfermline

Kirkcaldy

A16

Firth of Forth

Falkirk

C34

Dunbar

Cumbernauld

A13

Edinburgh

C30 C28

Livingston

A15 A17

Glasgow C29

A12

Key to Map A

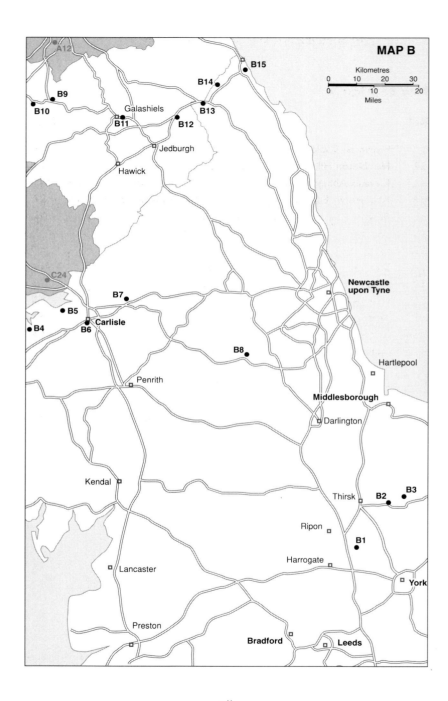

Key to Map B

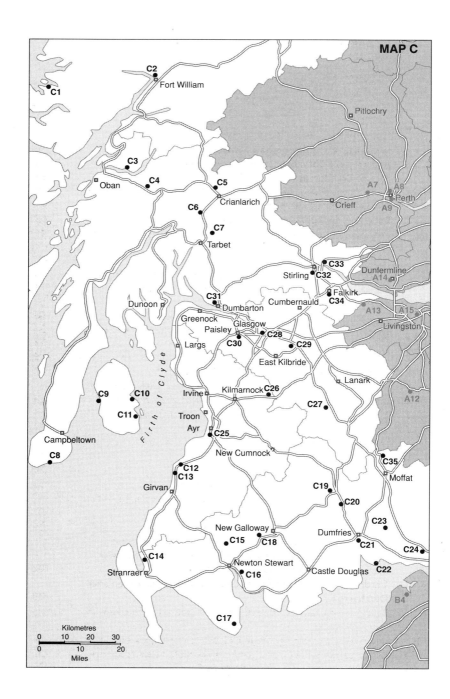

MAP C

C2
Fort William

C1

Pitlochry

C3

Oban
C4

C5
Crianlarich

C6

C7
Tarbet

A7
A8
Perth
Crieff
A9

C33
Stirling C32
Dunfermline
A14

Falkirk
Cumbernauld C34
A13
A15

Dunoon
C31
Dumbarton
Livingston

Greenock
Glasgow
Paisley
Largs
C30
C28

C29

East Kilbride

Lanark
A12

Firth of Clyde

C9
C10
Irvine
Kilmarnock C26

C11

C27

Troon
Ayr

Campbeltown
C25

C8
New Cumnock

C35

C12
Moffat
C13

Girvan
C19

C20

C23

New Galloway
Dumfries
C24

C15
C18
C21

C14
C22
Newton Stewart
Castle Douglas

Stranraer
C16

B4

C17

Kilometres
0   10   20   30
0   10   20
Miles

xiv

Key to Map C

Foreword

ROBERT THE BRUCE – of course I had heard of him – what Scottish youngster hadn't? I knew he had been king. I knew he was a patriot, even though I suppose I didn't really know the meaning of the word, but the ideal of it meant something to me. His name was mentioned at school, I remember that much. But the real depth of the life of this truly remarkable man was never discussed. He was a giant and he would have been a giant in any age. If his life was merely a story in a book, it would have been seen as a fantasy, a whim.

One day my mum came home with something from the Barras in Glasgow. (Barras is a corruption of Barrows, meaning wheeled stalls. It is the familiar, albeit somewhat glorified, name for a local Glasgow flea market.) She brought me a boxed set of three books, *The Bruce Trilogy* by Nigel Tranter. It lay around the house for a year or two. One day, when I was fourteen or fifteen, I was bored and picked it up, removed the first volume and began to read. It was the greatest story I had ever read.

The books were in the form of a novel. Did one man really do all that? Surely the work was mostly fiction? This form of history had made a boring subject come alive. Could these be real people on the page? Tranter's book made me read 'real' history books to cross-check situations, and I realised that, 700 years ago, Scotland would have ceased to exist had it not been for Bruce. He became my great hero. I started to visit sites with which he had an association. It became a bit of a hobby, and often on days out I would make a point of seeking out a site, if I could coerce my companions into doing so.

Wallace entered the story, then other characters from the Wars of Independence, eg, Douglas, Moray, Wishart and Lamberton. Sometimes Wallace came to the fore, sometimes Bruce. But it seems that this is the way the consciousness of Scotland is too. Bruce's star can be in the ascendancy, then Wallace's. In the late

20th century it is Wallace's time. *Braveheart*, the picture, is vivid in people's memories. But we are entering the era that marks the 700th anniversaries of many of Bruce's major milestones, so Bruce will rise again in the Scots' psyche. In the following pages I shall try to tell you his story and partly my story – how he has affected me, how I feel about some of the Bruce sites I have visited, and how he affects my Scotland.

Robert the Bruce, if only I could, I would ask you about Scotland and what it meant to you. Did you love it the way I love it? Ever since I was old enough to understand the concept of Scotland I have loved it, not really knowing why. Many of my peers cannot understand my passion, but I wonder if you felt it too, at a tender age. Wallace is different. I would not need to ask the question of him. I know he felt it. You are more the enigma. I just want to share your story with more people. This book is my attempt at doing just that.

David R Ross
May 1999

CHAPTER I

Origins and the Last Days of Peace

THE RUINS OF TURNBERRY CASTLE stand on the edge of the world-famous golf course of that name, on a low promontory washed on three sides by the sea. Only fragments of this once formidable fortress remain, but it has a claim to fame as being the probable birthplace of Robert I, The Bruce, the hero-king of Scots. (MAP C13)

It was built by the old Celtic Lords of Galloway, afterwards the Earls of Carrick – a title bestowed in 1186 by King William the Lion on Duncan, the grandson of Fergus of Galloway. Duncan's granddaughter married Robert Bruce, the father of our hero, in 1271, and as Countess of Carrick she brought the Earldom and the Castle under the Bruce family's control. Robert, the future king, was born on 11 July 1274 and Turnberry, his mother's home, would seem logical as his birthplace.

An access road runs directly west to Turnberry light-house from the A719 coast road. This lighthouse towers above the castle ruins. You can park and walk along the road through the golf course to have a look at the castle remains (beware low flying golf balls!). The view to Ailsa Craig will be the same as the one young Robert viewed. The rock pools below the ruins will be the ones he explored as a child. A cave beneath the castle opens up into the very core of the fortress. In its heyday this was probably a handy defensible access for supplies and weapons to come in from the sea.

Turnberry Castle

A little inland from Turnberry stands the village of Kirkoswald, and inside the ruined church is a font which is believed to have been used for Bruce's baptism. (MAP C12)

Font in Kirkoswald

As often happens in Scottish history, an alternative claim for Bruce's birthplace exists, and in this case it is for Lochmaben in Annandale, Dumfriesshire, a seat of the Bruce family. The manpower of fertile Annandale formed much of the strength of the Bruce faction in Scotland. In 1274 the castle in Lochmaben stood on top of the motte hill (a motte being a fortified mound, sometimes referred to as a moot-hill), at the side of the golf course, just to the west of the church.

The ruined castle which stands on a peninsula jutting into the Castle Loch a mile or so south-east of the motte was actually begun in 1298 by Edward I of England – 'Longshanks' – after his battle against Wallace at Falkirk, to try to consolidate his hold on south-west Scotland. The stones from the motte at the golf course would probably have been transferred to help with Edward's building programme. In later years, as Scotland once more regained her self-respect, the Bruce family would have claimed this castle which was built by Edward as their own.

There is an old local legend that a causeway had been constructed across the loch bed to help transfer the stones from one site to the other, but this would seem to be very unlikely, especially as the distance by water is not much different to that by land.

The later stone castle is now represented by mere fragments of once mighty walls and towers. Much of the facing stone has been robbed for other building work, and it is the interior rubble of the original walls that remains. The remnants of the moat on the landward side, however, are still very impressive. (MAP C23)

Although this castle has no connection with Bruce's place of birth, he would have been very familiar with it. It was besieged by him through August 1299, and attacked again in 1301. He captured it in 1306, only for it to be recaptured by the English, but after the victory at Bannockburn they finally surrendered it.

Bruce's connection with Lochmaben is commemorated by the statue of him which stands in the centre of the town, occupying the site of the old market cross. This statue, 8ft high, was created by John Hutchison RSA, and stands on a 10ft pedestal of Dalbeattie granite. It was unveiled on 13 September 1879.

Another Lochmaben Bruce connection is the parish church, built between 1818 and 1820, which contains two bells, one of which is said to have been a gift to King Robert the Bruce from the Pope.

Bruce Statue, Lochmaben

Who were the Bruces, and what were their origins? They had arrived in England as part of the Norman conquest of 1066. Their name originated from the town of Brix (there have been many spelling variations over the centuries, but this is the current one) near Cherbourg, where their stronghold was named Adam's Castle. This has long since disappeared, although books dating from the 1800s claimed that the odd foundation stone could still be located.

When King David I (1124-53) reigned in Scotland, he decided that some of these Normans, with their advanced weaponry and castle-building techniques, would be ideal for his northern realm, and he invited many north, giving them grants of lands in return for their services. One of the families was named Bruce, and was granted land in Annandale.

King Robert the Bruce was the seventh descendant of this first Lord of Annandale. Taking this into account, I am often surprised when I see claims which appear regularly that King Robert was not a Scot but some Norman-French overlord. If I were to suggest to people with surnames with a European flavour, such as

Denmark or Sorensen which show their ancestral origins, that they were in some way not Scots, even though their ancestors had been settled here for generations, I am sure they would be mightily offended. It should also be remembered that Bruce's mother was the wholly Celtic Countess of Carrick.

What does Norman mean? The word is actually a corruption of Northman or Norseman, these people having settled in Northern France some time before the conquest of England in 1066. So, do we take this matter to its extreme and call Bruce a Viking? We are all originally from somewhere else, but this fact seems to matter more to writers where Bruce is concerned. It is as if by questioning his heritage they somehow demean the man, as so many of our Scottish heroes have been demeaned over the years.

A letter appeared in the *Glasgow Herald* newspaper around 1995 claiming Bruce was 'Essex man'. This story that Bruce was born in England, or Essex to be more precise, is another of the misconceptions which I see once in a while. The story has its origins in the Chronicle of Geoffrey le Baker of Swinbrook who claimed Bruce's Essex birthplace. Others have copied this very unreliable source material, so the myth is perpetuated. A tradition that Bruce's father was perhaps born there would account for the origin of the story.

Bruce is mentioned in the Harcla Treaty of 1323, which states that 'Scotland has a king of its own nation'. Various English chronicles refer to Bruce as a Scot, and Bishop Wishart of Glasgow, when absolving him of the murder of the Red Comyn, refers to him as a 'layman of Carrick'.

What do we know of his upbringing? As the son of a baron he would have been instructed in the knightly arts. He obviously had a penchant for the battle-axe, since in later life he was regarded as a master of this murderous weapon. Used at different angles, it could cut, hack, slash or stun.

There has been debate over which language he would have spoken. Norman French would seem to have been the language of the upper classes. The locals around the south-western Bruce properties probably spoke Gaelic, the links with Ireland and the Isles still being very strong, so no doubt he would have been fluent in that too.

In recent times, Esperanto has been put forward as a universal language, in the hope that nation would be able to speak unto nation. People forget that such a language existed in medieval times. Latin was the language of the church, the bookkeepers and the scribes throughout western civilisation. A monk in, say, Argyll could pen a letter to France or Italy, and the monks there could fully comprehend it. No doubt a young lord would have picked up a few words and phrases from his tutors.

He would have travelled around the various Bruce properties, learning law and justice the hard way, as his father and grandfather had the power of life and death over wrongdoers.

Scotland in Bruce's boyhood years was a settled country under a strong king. However, this world was turned upside down when Bruce was eleven years old. King Alexander, the third to bear that name, was in his early forties, and had just married his second wife, Yolande. Although his children had predeceased him, the future looked reasonably bright. He already had one heir in his granddaughter Margaret, the Maid of Norway. Alexander's daughter had married the King of Norway, and the little girl, the product of this marriage, would be the queen of Scotland one day if Alexander's marriage to Yolande failed to produce any children.

King Alexander had been at Edinburgh Castle, and decided to return to his new bride Yolande, who was residing in the castle at Kinghorn in Fife. He hurried with an escort to Dalmeny, where the ferryman was roused and asked to take them across the Forth to Inverkeithing, even though it was a wild night.

The King was met at the far side by his master of the royal sauce-kitchen, who asked him not to travel further, but the King could not be persuaded. He set off for Kinghorn and disappeared in the night. Next morning he was found on the shore at the bottom of a cliff, his neck broken. The spot is marked by a monument erected in 1886 which stands between the cliffs and the sand, on the south side of the coast road between Burtisland and Kinghorn, at Pettycur Bay. (MAP A16)

One of Scotland's oldest pieces of poetry has its origins in this event:

> When Alexander our King was dead
> That Scotland led in love and law
> Away was sons (plenty) of ale and bread
> Of wine and wax, of game and glee
> Our gold was changed into lead
> Christ, born in virginity
> Succour Scotland and remedy
> That State is in perplexity.

Alexander was buried in Dunfermline Abbey, where his first wife Margaret, sister of Edward, King of England, had been interred.

Queen Yolande was said to be with child, but it was wishful thinking. The new monarch was to be the Maid of Norway, a little girl of seven, not a ideal successor to Alexander, as Scotland required a strong male ruler to keep the nobles under control.

Edward I, the late King's brother-in-law, saw a way to unite Scotland with England. His son, Edward, would marry the Maid of Norway. He sent a ship to Norway to collect her. At the same time he took control of the Isle of Man, a Scottish possession, and more sinisterly, named the warlike Bishop of Durham, Anthony Beck, as Lieutenant of Scotland in Prince Edward and the Maid's name, even though they were neither married nor had their intended marriage been sanctioned by the government in Scotland.

Erik II of Norway, the Maid's father, declined Edward's offer to carry the Maid over the sea, preferring her to sail in one of his own vessels. However, in October 1290, on her way to Scotland, the Maid died in Orkney. Her body was taken back to Bergen for burial in the cathedral. The cathedral was demolished many years ago, but the Maid and several other Norwegian monarchs are commemorated by a plaque near the site of the old cathedral.

How different Scotland would have been if the Maid had survived. How Erik must have grieved for this little girl, who was Queen of Scots, yet never reigned over or even saw Scotland – Orkney at that time still being under the sway of Norway.

Who was now to rule Scotland? Thirteen claimants came forward, all with a seeming right to be King of Scots. The monarch in Scotland has always been King or Queen of Scots, whereas in England the monarch was King or Queen of England. The subtlety of this must be explained. The King in Scotland was king by the acknowledgement of the twelve premier earls, and therefore, in theory at least, by the decision of the people. He was King of Scots, not of Scotland, whereas in England, the monarch's power was more absolute, thus King of England.

There was no obvious heir to the Scottish throne. We have to trace the royal line back to the time of Malcolm the Maiden, or his brother William the Lion. These two had left no heirs, but they had a younger brother, David, Earl of Huntingdon, who had three daughters. A certain John Balliol was grandson of the eldest daughter, and Robert Bruce (the grandfather of our hero) was son of the second daughter. These two had the most legitimate argument of the thirteen claimants, and as they had the largest contingents of followers in the country, the threat of civil war hung over the land.

The Balliols were Lords of Galloway. John Balliol was probably born at Kenmure Castle, the later ruins of which still stand on top of the mound at the north end of Loch Ken, just south of New Galloway. The mound looks to be man–made, but closer inspection reveals rock strata at the top, showing it is a quirk of nature. The Castle, renovated several times, contains some ancient vaults in its core. It was still inhabited in the latter part of the 20th century, as a television aerial stuck on a wallhead the last time I visited it testifies.

Balliol was the son of Devorgilla of Galloway, the founder of Balliol College in Oxford. She built the old bridge over the Nith in Dumfries. It originally had nine arches, but only six survive, which is why access is now by a flight of stone steps. The bridge, which Robert the Bruce would have used, shows where the main thoroughfare ran through Dumfries in Bruce's time. She was more famously responsible for the building of Sweetheart Abbey. Her husband, John Balliol senior, Lord of Galloway, had died in 1269 at Barnard Castle in England. When she died in 1290 at the age of eighty, her body, according to her direction, was buried in New Abbey with her late husband's embalmed heart placed against hers, in a rich tomb before the high altar. The name Dulce Cor, or Sweetheart Abbey, has been applied to the place ever since. Its ruins stand seven or eight miles south of Dumfries, under Criffel Hill.

The Bruces, by coincidence near neighbours of the Balliols, held the title Lord of Annandale. Robert Bruce, the grandfather of King Robert the Bruce was known as 'The Competitor' due to his competing with Balliol for the throne. If Balliol had tried to mount the throne of Scotland, it would have been bitterly contested by the Bruces, and vice versa, not to mention the outcry from some of the other claimants. Only one person could choose a king, and that was another king.

In a bid to stop an escalation into bloodshed, Bishop Fraser of St Andrews wrote to Edward Longshanks asking for his intervention. There was no lack of patriotism in this act; after all, Edward had been brother-in-law to the late King Alexander and had been ready to marry his son to the Maid of Norway. The snatching of the Isle of Man, among other incidents, had not really impressed itself on the Scots, and Edward happily came north to pick the rightful heir.

Norham Castle

He reached Norham Castle on the English side of the Tweed in May 1291. (MAP B14)

From the first it was obvious the Bruce and Balliol claims were the only two with any real chance. Balliol was descended from the elder daughter of the Earl of Huntingdon, so he thought that gave him the greater claim. Not necessarily, claimed Bruce. Balliol was a grandson, whereas he was a son and therefore had a greater right by being closer in line, even though he stemmed from the younger daughter. Bruce the Competitor also claimed that Alexander had made a promise to him during his reign that, should he die without lawful issue, Bruce would inherit the throne.

Edward and various judges sat to ponder the situation. The true nature of Edward's intentions started to become apparent, however, when he insisted that the claimants would have to acknowledge him as their Lord Paramount, and demanded various Scottish castles 'so that he could confer them on to the rightful heir'. Unfortunately, ambition overrode right thinking, and the claimants agreed to this, each scared that the other would gain an advantage.

I wonder what was going through the future King Robert's mind at this time. He had turned seventeen, and he would know that if his grandfather was chosen as the rightful king, he would be second in line to inherit the throne. Robert had several siblings, his brothers Edward, Nigel, Thomas and Alexander, and sisters Mary and Christian.

A decision was finally reached, and Edward of England decreed that Balliol was the rightful King of Scots. The Bruce family would not have taken this news with good grace. They retired to their castles and keeps, and we can picture the recriminations and talk of the future around the dinner tables.

Balliol began his reign in 1292. From the first, Edward regarded him with disdain, making various demands on him and treating him as his junior, rather than as an equal and the king of a neigh-bouring independent nation. The nobles of Scotland began to fear Edward's motives – they could see the gathering of the storm clouds. After all, he had recently annexed Wales, creating his son the first Prince of Wales.

The crunch came when Edward demanded that Balliol should raise a Scottish army to go and fight in England's continental wars. The Scots then took a stand, signing a treaty with France against English aggression. (This was the beginning of the Auld Alliance between Scotland and France that each should use the other to counter the English threat.) Edward was outraged. He saw Scotland as a vassal kingdom, and decided the Scots needed to be taught a lesson.

The year was 1296.

CHAPTER 2

War Begins

AT THE END OF the 13th century the armies of England were the mightiest fighting machines in Christendom. In Edward Plantagenet England had its most ambitious and ruthless king – at least when it came to expanding his borders. (With regard to that last statement I started to think about Queen Victoria and the British Empire, so I will talk about Edward's effect on his neighbouring nations, rather than expansion on a global scale.)

Edward was born at Westminster on 17 June 1239. As a grown man, he stood 6ft 2ins tall. English chronicles mention that he stood almost 7ft in his armour and war-helm – an exceptional height for the times. He had blond hair which turned white in older age. Nearly all contemporaries mention that he had a drooping eyelid, and he was usually depicted as clean shaven.

While still a young man, he fought two battles for his father, Henry III. One was at Lewes near Brighton, where although the King's army was beaten, he won his part of the battle; the other was at Evesham, where the royal troops were victorious.

The more one delves into Edward's character, the more unsavoury he appears. He would promise one thing, then do another. Anything which he reckoned would be to his gain was considered fair. Edward practised endlessly in the lists for tournaments, and was said to be recklessly brave at these events.

In August 1270 he went on crusade, and while he was away his father died. He returned home to be crowned King, and the coronation took place in August 1274. After his coronation, he turned to the complete annexation of Wales. He was constantly at war in France. It was only a matter of time before he looked towards Scotland.

Edward's personal ambitions destroyed the peace between

England and Scotland. Seven hundred years on, Scotsmen still eye Englishmen with suspicion. This was Edward's legacy. He started a war that left tens of thousands dead. The first stage of the war lasted thirty-two years. In the end Scotland won. Little Scotland outfought and outmaneouvered Edward. He could never have envisaged that. The Scots are generally too busy fighting amongst themselves to bother about what is going on around them. But when the threat reaches crisis point, they can usually be relied upon to form a united front – and even win, if the leadership is there in quality.

Edward brought his great army north and entered Scotland by crossing the Tweed fords at Coldstream. If you stand on the area of grassland between the village and the river, just east of the stream entering the Tweed, you are on the spot where the War of Independence actually began. Locals who take part in Coldstream's civic week which involves a ride-out to Flodden Battlefield, until recently crossed the river here and know of the existence of the fords. (MAP B13)

The army then turned east and made its way downstream to Berwick, the greatest town at that time in Scotland, doing rich trade with Europe. Berwick had a vast income in revenues, and Edward had probably cast covetous eyes upon it for many years. Scotland and England had been reasonable neighbours and the town walls were in some disrepair. (MAP B15)

Edward's army smashed its way into the town and began to slaughter men, women and children in the streets. Of the population of 20,000, probably some 15,000 died. The captain commanding the castle at Berwick was captured and taken south. He was William Douglas, and had already fathered a son, James, who was to become a warrior whose name was enough to make Englishmen shake in their boots.

When at Flodden in 1995, I spoke to some Berwick folk about the Sack of Berwick, as it came to be known. They had never heard of it. This part of history has been suppressed. Realising that March 1996 was the 700th anniversary of the event, I wrote an article for the local Berwick press, in the hope that the year, and the innocents who had lost their lives, could somehow be commemorated. The date of the anniversary came and went and the item was never used. Berwick today is an English town with about 12,000 inhabitants.

Very little remains in Berwick from these times, but at the railway station, opposite the platforms, there are remnants of walls which are all that remain of the castle of the late 1200s. Some sections of the old town walls run from the castle remains down to the River Tweed.

The Scots had assembled an army at Caddonlea further upstream on the River Tweed. The English army moved north along Scotland's eastern coast and started to besiege Dunbar Castle. The Scots caught them there. As the English left the siege area to attack, the Scots, who were badly led and had no experience of war, gave the high ground to come to grips with the enemy. The English broke up to cross the ravine of the Spott burn, and the Scots in their naivety thinking they were fleeing, spurred forward piecemeal only to be routed in minutes with the English regrouping in good battle order.

The site of this opening battle of the War of Independence is marked on modern OS maps in the fields north of the Spott burn, just east of Spott village itself.

Scotland now lay open to major invasion. Most of its senior nobles had been routed or captured. King John Balliol fled north and hid in the glens of the North and South Esk. Edward and his armies followed. Balliol was captured and brought before Edward in the churchyard at Stracathro, north of Brechin, where he was forced to renounce his treaty with France.

The little church at Strathcathro stands on the site of more ancient buildings. It is a mile west of the A90, on the far side of Stracathro Hospital.

As far as Edward was concerned, this was the end of Scotland as a nation. In future it was just to be a northern extension of his realm. The following day, 8 July 1296, Balliol was stripped of his crown and Lion Rampant surcoat in Montrose. The loss of the surcoat gave rise to his nickname, 'Toom Tabard', or 'empty coat'. This event probably took place at the castle of Montrose, represented today by a building known as the Castle Stead which stands on the site of the original castle. When workmen in Montrose were digging the foundations for the Hume Monument in the High Street in 1859, they discovered a coin hoard containing nineteen silver coins of Edward's reign, along with other objects. These were probably hidden at the time of Edward's visit.

After sending Balliol south to an English prison, then eventual exile to his family lands in France, Edward continued north, travelling as far as Elgin before proceeding southwards again. At Berwick he demanded that all the major landowners come and sign a document of fealty to him. Seeing what Edward had done to Berwick would leave them in no doubt about his power. Many Scots would doubtless have strong patriotic feelings, and would see themselves as being forced under duress to add their names to the document; but many were willing to sign, doing whatever they thought would push their interests to the fore.

This document became known as the 'Ragman Roll' – a reference to the state of the Scots who had signed it, hence the word 'rigmarole' – something time-consuming and worthless.

Edward had looted a great deal during his progress through Scotland, and when he re-crossed the Tweed into England, he took with him what he believed to be the Stone of Destiny, the ancient crowning chair of the Kings of Scots. The Holy Rood of St Margaret, said to be a piece of the true cross on which Christ was crucified and a talisman for the Scots, was also removed. Edward took these to show that the nation no longer existed. He also took many historical documents which was a great loss to Scotland, as very little hard documentation exists from these early times.

Edward thought he had left a defeated country behind him, but instead this was the start of the era when the men who were to become Scotland's national heroes would arise.

What do we know of Robert, the future king, during the time

of Balliol? In 1292 his father, the son of the Competitor, resigned the Earldom of Carrick to him, basically so that he did not have to take an oath of fealty to John Balliol which would have jeopardised his family's claim to the throne. So, at the age of eighteen, Robert was promoted to one of the great Earldoms of Scotland.

The Competitor died in 1295 at Lochmaben Castle, and his son, Robert's father, assumed the title of Lord of Annandale. The Competitor would appear to have been made of sterner stuff than his son. Perhaps he had seen some of the grit that his grandson was to show in life, allowing him to die knowing the Bruce lineage was in safe hands. After the Battle of Dunbar, young Robert asked Edward for the crown of Scotland as Balliol had openly defied England. Edward sarcastically replied, 'Have we nothing to do but win kingdoms for you?' before turning his back. Robert, the future king, must have felt a dreadful embarrassment at this.

The next few years were to be a hard school for Scotland. Bruce was to be a pupil at this school, and was to learn what real courage and devotion were all about. His teacher was William Wallace.

CHAPTER 3

The Wallace Years

AT SOME TIME DURING THE Balliol era, Robert had married. Examining the family ties, it was probably an arranged marriage. His bride was Isabel, daughter of the Earl of Mar who had been close to his grandfather, the Competitor. We know very little about Isabel, but of importance for the future was that she bore Robert a daughter, Marjorie. We do not know Marjorie's date of birth, but it was certainly before 1297. Isabel died around this time, and she must have still been little more than a girl. Perhaps she died in childbirth or from some complication deriving from her confinement.

Edward had left Scotland feeling it was a cowed land, and went off to France to push England's claims there. No sooner was he away than Scotland shook itself and began to find some pride again. In the south of Scotland a young giant of a man slew the English sheriff of Lanark, perhaps in retribution for the murder of his sweetheart, and young men flocked to his banner. His name was William Wallace. In the north, Andrew Murray raised his standard at Avoch in the Black Isle, and began to clear the castles of their English garrisons.

Robert Bruce, following English orders, made a raid on Douglas Castle in Lanarkshire, but he suddenly turned against his foreign overlords and declared himself in favour of the Scottish cause. The story goes that he delivered Lady Douglas and her children to William Douglas, the keeper of the castle at the Sack of Berwick who had slipped his English leash and escaped. Among William Douglas's children was his eldest, James, who would never forget how Robert saved his family from the English.

Many theories have been espoused over the years regarding Bruce's actions at this time. The English chronicler, Walter of

Guisborough, states that, 'Bruce joined the Scots because he was a Scotsman'. It was probably that simple. He would certainly have had misgivings because many of the Scots freedom-fighters acted in the name of the absent John Balliol whom Bruce would never regard as king, as this stood in the way of his own family's claims.

Bruce was joined by Robert Wishart, Bishop of Glasgow, and the Stewart – as the High Steward of Scotland was more commonly known. Henry Percy and Robert Clifford, two of Edward of England's foremost captains, raised an army from the northern English shires, and marched north to counter the threat. They halted at Ayr, with the Scots based at Irvine a few miles north. The Scots immediately employed stalling tactics, arguing about Edward's earlier demands for a Scots army to serve abroad and claiming that this was the cause of much of the current discontent. This delay proved vital to events elsewhere, with Wallace and Murray both gaining strength from the pause in proceedings.

The Scots at Irvine parleyed for peace, and it was demanded that Bruce should hand over his daughter, Marjorie, as surety for his future behaviour. He did not hand over his daughter, though, playing a game of cat and mouse instead. William Douglas was recaptured and taken south, to be kept in close confinement till the hostages the English demanded were handed over. He was eventually to die in the Tower of London, and his son James, though still a boy, was to make a vow to regain all that his father had lost. He was thereafter raised in Paris to keep him from Edward's clutches. He believed his father had been murdered while in prison.

The Scots under Wallace and Murray were besieging the English garrison of the castle at Dundee when word arrived of an English army coming north under the Earl of Warenne, assisted by Edward's Treasurer of Scotland, one Hugh Cressingham.

To reach the northern part of Scotland, it was obvious that this army would have to cross the bridge over the Forth at Stirling. The Scots, led by Wallace and Murray, met them there on 11 September 1297, charging from the Abbey Craig where the National Wallace Monument now stands. The English heavy cavalry could not deploy out on the soft ground on either side of the causeway that led from the end of the bridge, and the Scots cut the English chivalry to pieces.

This battle must have had a huge effect on the minds of Scots and English alike as the news spread. Scots would have realised that they had the ability to defy Edward's expansionist policy, but the greater shock would have been felt in the south, where Englishmen would have heard the news of their army's defeat with disbelieving ears. It would have been astonishing for them to learn that their well-equipped army of gentlemen soldiers had been annihilated by what was to them little more than a rabble of peasantry, one of the leaders a mere second son of a minor knight. Wallace was dealt a major blow, however, as Murray suffered a wound in this battle that was eventually to prove fatal.

We have no idea of Bruce's whereabouts while the Battle of Stirling Bridge took place. It would be interesting to know what his reaction was on hearing the news of the victory. His natural patriotism for his native soil would have been offset by the fact that Wallace acted in the name of the absent John Balliol – an obvious choice for Wallace, as Balliol was the name he needed to use to legitimise his struggle. Bruce would have worried about how this would affect his family's claim. His father, meanwhile, had accepted Edward of England's captaincy of Carlisle, which must have put his mind in a whirl, not only giving him concerns for his country's situation, but complicating matters where family ties were concerned.

After the victory in September, Wallace launched a raid into northern England, sending booty and livestock back into Scotland, but the early onset of a hard winter cut this invasion rather short. Sometime around the end of 1296 and the beginning of 1297 Wallace was knighted and created Guardian of Scotland. This took place most likely at the Kirk of the Forest, the remains of which still stand in Selkirk, which in those times was in the heart of the Ettrick Forest, hence the name.

Around this time, Bruce's father retired from public life, perhaps due to English pressure regarding his son's position among the Scots 'rebels'.

Edward Longshanks, of course, was not going to put up with what he saw as insurrection in his northern realm, and he mustered an army to return north and teach Wallace a lesson.

On 22 July 1298, the two armies met above the Westquarter Burn at Falkirk. The Scots were grouped in huge spear rings, known as 'schiltroms'. Not having the power of knighted cavalry that England could muster, the Scots devised a hedgehog formation of spearmen as a way to counter the horsemen. In the days before artillery, physical contact had to be made to injure the enemy. The English horsemen charged time and time again against the schiltroms, but the massed spearmen held.

The Scots did have cavalry at Falkirk, but they fled the field at the onset of battle. Several theories have been put forward for this. One was that the mounted gentlemen of Scotland were jealous of Wallace's elevated position in their ranks, and refused to fight for him. Another was that it was merely cowardice against what seemed overwhelming odds. Much has also been made of the fact that one of the leaders of the cavalry was John Comyn the Red, whom Bruce was later to slay at Dumfries. Later Scots chroniclers have blamed Comyn for the departure of the cavalry, to portray him in as bad a light as possible in order to further the Bruce legend.

The Scots spearmen were able to withstand the repeated cavalry charges until Edward brought forward a section of his army which the schiltroms had no answer for, the longbowmen. They fired into the massed spearmen, and, as the rings started to disintegrate, the renewed cavalry charges were able to break into the interior of the Scots' positions and wreak havoc from within. Falkirk was won and lost.

Wallace managed to escape from the carnage. We do not know if Bruce was present at Falkirk, but the tactics employed by the Scots were a learning process for him. He knew that the English cavalry could not break the ranks of the Scots spearmen, but the Scots needed horsemen to counter the threat from the English longbow. Bruce would remember this and he would use the lesson to great effect in the latter stages of the war.

Much has been written regarding Bruce's whereabouts during the battle. A later biographer of Wallace, Blind Harry, says that Bruce fought alongside the English at Falkirk. (Blind Harry's tale of the life of William Wallace was the basis for the picture *Braveheart,* hence the reason Bruce was portrayed in the film as fighting with Edward's forces.)

According to Blind Harry, Wallace and Bruce met after the battle at Dunipace, and Wallace berated Bruce for taking the side of their foe. Dunipace (the location of the more modern town of Dunipace has moved over the centuries) stood where the Hills of Dunipace cemetery now lies, alongside the River Carron. But this meeting would seem to be fantasy, since after the battle Edward of England advanced on Ayr, only to find the castle had been fired by Bruce – not something one would expect if they had fought side-by-side only weeks before. (MAP C25)

There is an ongoing campaign to portray Bruce as somehow underhand. Articles appear in newspapers on a regular basis portraying Bruce as a scheming self-seeker who changed sides as it suited him. This view has been constantly exploded by historians and writers, but it still seems to have a hold in popular imagination. Barron's book on the Wars of Independence, published in 1914, shows the nonsense of these claims, and most writers since, most notably G.W.S. Barrow in his book on Bruce, show the quality of Bruce's aims and standpoints. But the negative depiction of Bruce still exists, probably espoused by the more unionist of Scotland – the old divide-and-rule situation.

I have been asked if I think Wallace and Bruce ever met. I consider it to be highly likely they would have known each other reasonably well. They would be near each other in age. We know Bruce was born in 1274. Wallace's birthdate is uncertain, but is reckoned to have been between 1270 and 1274, so Wallace was perhaps the elder, but only by a year or two.

After the battle at Falkirk, William Lamberton arrived back in

Scotland from Rome, having been consecrated Bishop of St Andrews. He and Bishop Robert Wishart of Glasgow became the epitome of the church militant. They tirelessly fought for Scotland's freedom, preaching the cause from their pulpits, and came to symbolise the individualism of the church in Scotland.

Wallace resigned his post as Guardian of Scotland soon after Falkirk, obviously deeply affected by the death of so many of his fellows. From then until his death seven years later in 1305, he strove constantly to further Scotland's interests. After his resignation, new Guardians were appointed – Robert Bruce and John Comyn the Red. Bruce, who was one of the foremost nobles in Scotland, was for many people the true heir to the throne of Scotland. The fact that he was elected Guardian surely shows that the story that he fought with the English at Falkirk only weeks before is nonsense.

John Comyn, or Cumming as he would be called today, was known as 'the Red' to differentiate him from his uncle John, who was known as John the Black. John the Red was Lord of Badenoch, and the Comyns collectively were probably the most powerful family in Scotland circa 1300. They had blood ties with the recently deposed Balliol, and although John the Red had apparently deserted the Scots at Falkirk, the Comyns generally fought hard for Scotland's liberty. Unfortunately, the Comyns and the Bruces, even when fighting on the same side, seem to have behaved very much like two dogs eyeing the same bone. But, putting their differences aside or possibly because they were the two main families in Scotland, Comyn and Bruce became Guardians together with Lamberton, the Bishop of St Andrews.

Wallace, meanwhile, travelled abroad to put Scotland's cause before the King of France. He may also have travelled to Rome to try to elicit help from the Pope. A letter survives which was sent to King Edward at this time giving an insight, not only into the relationship between Bruce and Comyn, but also into that which may have existed between Bruce and Wallace. The letter was forwarded from a spy who had been present at a meeting in the

Peebles area, where a certain Sir David Graham had made a demand for the property of Sir William Wallace who was going abroad without asking the consent of the Guardians. William's brother, Sir Malcolm Wallace, was present at the meeting and made an objection to Graham's demands. Graham and Wallace drew their daggers, confronting each other. (MAP B9)

Graham was of Comyn's following and Wallace was of Bruce's following. It was reported to John Comyn and his uncle, the Earl of Buchan, that this fight had broken out. Comyn leapt at Bruce, seizing him by the throat, while Buchan turned on Bishop Lamberton. Comyn and Buchan accused Bruce and Lamberton of treason, but others who were present, including the Stewart, came between them and calmed the situation. Comyn had immediately blamed Bruce; Lamberton was seen as Bruce's accomplice; and, intriguingly, Wallace's elder brother was seen to be a member of Bruce's following. Lamberton, in all likliehood, was the man behind Wallace's sojourn abroad, and it is interesting to note that Bruce was regarded as being Lamberton's associate in what happened. A young man with Bruce's pride and upbringing would not readily forget Comyn's mishandling of him. After the gathering broke up, Lamberton remained in the Peebles area at his manor of Stobo, a few miles upstream on the Tweed. Bruce headed southwest to attack the English-held castle of Lochmaben, and John the Red and Buchan returned to their lands in the north-east.

Some time after this, Bruce resigned as Guardian. This may have been connected with the altercation with the Red Comyn. Comyn and Lamberton remained as Guardians and were joined by Sir Ingram de Unfraville.

In mid summer 1300 the Scots held a parliament in Rutherglen. The castle at Rutherglen stood at what is now the junction between Castle Street and King Street. It was demolished in the early 1700s. A remnant of the 14th century survives in the ruin of the old church, with a later tower, which stands in the old cemetery at the side of Rutherglen Town Hall.

At the same time as the parliament was taking place, Edward

of England mustered an invasion force at Carlisle. He advanced along the Solway coast, relieved Lochmaben Castle, then laid siege to Caerlaverock. Confronted by the huge force, the captain of Caerlaverock Castle asked for terms for surrender. Edward was outraged, viewing the garrison as traitors, and refused terms, bringing up siege engines which made short work of the castle. In one of his famous rages, he had the entire garrison hung.

The impressive ruins of Caerlaverock stand on a triangular island in a moat in Lochar Moss, east of the River Nith, a few miles south of Dumfries. (MAP C22)

Advancing west, the English army met a force of Scots under the Red Comyn and Buchan, and a running fight took place between Creetown and Newton Stewart. When the English cavalry started to deploy, the Scots broke up in disorder, each man making his escape as best he could. Although this was an obvious victory for Edward, he was unable to push the advantage, and crossed back over the border in autumn 1300, declaring that he would waste all of Scotland and force its people into submission. (MAP C16)

At the end of the year the remaining Guardians resigned and a new Guardian, John de Soules, Lord of Liddesdale, took on the mantle.

Soules' castle of Hermitage still towers over Liddesdale, a gaunt giant of a place and a remnant of lordly power.

Hermitage Castle

Soules was fairly neutral when it came to the Comyn-Balliol/Bruce factions. Various machinations were taking place between the Vatican and the King of France, putting pressure on Edward of England to recognise Scotland's sovereignty, and to restore John Balliol as monarch. This news must have caused much heart searching in Robert Bruce.

Edward of England made another effort to overrun Scotland in 1301, when he planned a pincer movement across southern Scotland, intending to meet up with a western invasion force, commanded by his son, Prince Edward, at Inverkip on the Clyde, but although this force managed to take Turnberry Castle and Bothwell Castle, the two armies finally met at Linlithgow where they decided to spend the winter.

We know that Bruce had been actively thwarting English ambitions in the west of Scotland. However, that winter there was news that a restoration of Balliol was possible; worse still, from Bruce's point of view, was the fact that lands owned by people active in service against England were to be handed over to the King of France until Balliol was reinstated, at which time the lands would be parcelled out again. Bruce realised that this would mean he could lose not only his believed right to the throne, but also his Earldom of Carrick.

A truce was drawn up between the Scots and Edward, under pressure from France, and Bruce, obviously after much soul-searching, decided to make his peace with Edward. This was done in the knowledge that, as a truce was in operation, he was not reneging on his fellows. He was aware that Edward, already old for that day and age, could not live much longer, and that his son was not of the same mould as his father. As all power stemmed from land ownership, Bruce needed to hold on to the vast estates of his inheritance to have any hope for the future. When his father died, he would inherit the Lordship of Annandale.

Another reason for his peace-making which has been the subject of debate and is certainly relevant might have been his marriage to Elizabeth de Burgh, daughter of the Anglo-Irish Earl of Ulster.

Over the next few years, Bruce is rarely mentioned in documentation because he did not take the field against Edward, or play much of a part in the politics of Scotland.

Resistance carried on against the English. Wallace returned from his foreign travels some time in 1303. On 24 February 1303, an English force was surprised and attacked by an army of Scots at Roslin, south of Edinburgh. The Scots were led by the Red Comyn and Sir Simon Fraser, a comrade of Wallace, and the English suffered a heavy defeat. The battle is said to have taken place on the moor of Roslin, to the north of the old town. (MAP A12)

Edward came north again in person, seeking revenge. He was supported by troops from Ireland, who took Rothesay Castle, the ruins of which, complete to the wallhead, still stand in the centre of Rothesay. They then went to Inverkip, which by its mention in various documents was an important stronghold. There is no longer any trace of this fortress, but it undoubtedly was where a later tower house stands on the ridge, today covered in woodland, that runs back from Ardgowan House, half a mile north of modern Inverkip village.

Edward made for the north-east and besieged various castles, and after reaching Kinloss in September 1303, he turned south to winter at Dunfermline, where he again displayed his ruthlessness of character. When he left Dunfermline early in 1304, he had the abbey buildings put to the torch, even though they contained the tomb of his sister Margaret, who had been Alexander III's Queen.

In February 1304, a force almost captured Wallace at Happrew, a few miles west of Peebles. Since his return from abroad, Wallace had been fighting a guerrilla war to the best of his ability, but the odds were becoming longer all the time.

Stirling Castle was still in the hands of the Scots, and in May Edward started to besiege it with every means at his disposal. It was defended manfully by Sir William Oliphant, and a plaque in the Castle commemorates his outstanding defence of his charge. The garrison at Stirling finally submitted on 20 July, but Edward characteristically would not let them leave until he had brought forward his most modern siege engine, called the Warwolf. The defenders had to suffer further bombardment from this device until 24 July, when Edward had the fifty or so survivors march out in sackcloth to be sent south to English prisons.

By this time, seeing that Edward's star was very much in the ascendancy, almost all the Scots leadership had come into his peace. A peace treaty signed between England and France had pushed Balliol once more into the political wilderness, as he was no longer a useful pawn to be used to bring pressure to bear on Scotland from France.

Eventually only Wallace was still on the offensive, but his end came the following year in early August 1305, when he was captured at Robroyston near Glasgow with a single companion, Kerlie, who was slain on the spot. The barn where he was caught was destroyed many years ago, but the site is marked with a beautiful monument in the style of a Celtic cross erected in 1900.

He was taken south and paraded through various towns as an object of ridicule and derision, before reaching London. The following day, 23 August, he was dragged behind horses for five miles through the streets, before suffering the hideous death of torture, disembowellment and finally beheading. His body was quartered and sent for display in various cities as a warning of Edward's terrible power. The site of his execution is marked by a plaque on the wall of St Bartholomew's Hospital, where it overlooks the square at West Smithfield.

Wallace must have died thinking there was no-one left in Scotland who offered the kind of defiance that he demonstrated so well. He could never have envisaged what fate had in store for Bruce, Earl of Carrick, but he had blazed a trail of glory which would shine throughout Scottish history, and in time Bruce would follow a similar path.

CHAPTER 4

The Man who would be King

BRUCE'S FATHER DIED SOMETIME in 1304 in the Carlisle area, and was buried in the Abbey of Holm Cultram in Abbeytown, about eighteen miles south-west of Carlisle. His tombstone survives and stands in the porch of the Abbey. With his death, Bruce was now not only Earl of Carrick and Lord of Annandale, but had become, in his own mind, rightful heir to the throne of his country. (MAP B4)

Although he had nominally made his peace with England, we know that plans for subterfuge were taking shape in Bruce's mind. He had signed a bond with Bishop Lamberton, worded somewhat enigmatically saying that they had entered a mutual alliance to defend each other against potential enemies or else forfeit a penalty of £10,000. The wording is rather vague, but reading between the lines of this document which was drawn up at Cambuskenneth Abbey on 11 June 1304, we can see that Bruce and Lamberton must have been having serious discussions regarding Scotland's future – and Bruce's part in it.

Cambuskenneth figured largely in the Wars of Independence, and it was there that the spoils of the Battle of Bannockburn were shared out. It is the burial place of James III of Scotland and his Queen.

Cambuskenneth Abbey is represented today by scant ruins, overlooked by a more or less complete bell-tower. The gargoyles around the top of the tower are a notable curiosity. The ruins stand in a loop of the River Forth opposite Stirling,

Cambuskenneth Abbey

and are approached by a road running from the Abbey Craig, the scene of Wallace's victory at Stirling Bridge. In Wallace and Bruce's time there was a ford across the Forth near the Abbey. The National Wallace Monument stands on top of the Abbey Craig (or crag), so-called because of its proximity to Cambuskenneth.

The ruins are looked after by Historic Scotland, and the gate is generally unlocked during daylight hours. Cambuskenneth village is connected to Stirling by means of a footbridge over the river.

The month after Wallace's execution, when the last bastion of resistance against English occupation had fallen, Edward drew up a document with various points for the running of Scotland known as the Ordinance of 1305. It contains the following words:

> It is agreed that the Earl of Carrick shall be commanded to put Kildrummy Castle in the keeping of such a man as he himself will be willing to answer for.

This seems to imply that Edward was not altogether sure of Bruce. Edward would not have known of his secret bond with Lamberton. However, Wishart and Lamberton were friends of Wallace and of Bruce. We know from English records that when Wallace was captured he had various papers with him (which are unfortunately lost to us), and it is possible that some of these may have cast doubt on Bruce.

The powderkeg finally exploded in February 1306 when Bruce stabbed the Red Comyn to death and assumed the Crown of Scotland. Bruce may have done this in a fit of passion – knowing that such a deed would not only create all out war with England, but would also incur the wrath of the Comyn and Balliol factions in Scotland, which would basically result in civil war.

Scottish chronicles all tell the same story about the lead-up to these events. Apparently Bruce drew up a document for himself and the Red Comyn, stating that Bruce would grant Comyn all his lands if he would help him become King and resume the nation's fight against England. Comyn informed King Edward of Bruce's planned 'treachery'. The Earl of Gloucester, a friend of Bruce, sent him a pair of spurs and a shilling as a warning. Bruce got the message and used the shilling to tip the messenger, then immediately galloped for the border.

Two English sources mention that Bruce approached Comyn, one version being that Comyn could have Bruce's lands in exchange for backing for the throne, and the other that Bruce accused Comyn of betraying him to Edward. Whatever the truth, we know that Bruce and Comyn met in the Greyfriars monastery which stood in the centre of Dumfries. An argument broke out, perhaps because Comyn had betrayed Bruce and was being confronted with the evidence, or perhaps it was simply mutual dislike, as evidenced by Comyn's earlier mishandling of Bruce at Peebles. Harsh words were spoken which resulted in Bruce drawing his dagger and stabbing Comyn. In the heat of the moment, Bruce must have forgotten that he was in a religious building and had stabbed Comyn in front of the altar – an act of supreme sacrilege. Sir Robert Comyn, the uncle of the victim, ran forward to protect him, but was struck dead with a blow to the head from the sword of Sir Christopher Seton, who was married to Bruce's sister Christian.

A strong tradition survives that Bruce did not strike the fatal blow to Comyn, and that he was lying wounded when Roger Kirkpatrick of Closeburn uttered the phrase, 'I mak siccar' (I make sure) and dispatched him. This phrase is now the motto of the Kirkpatricks.

Closeburn Castle

The Kirkpatricks inhabited Closeburn Castle until 1783, when it was sold. The Castle has undergone many changes, but still retains its main keep from the late 1300s. Closeburn is a private residence, but it can be seen from the A76, a couple of miles south of Thornhill in Dumfriesshire. (MAP C20)

The scant remains of Tibbers Castle north-west of Thornhill are worth a visit. (MAP C19) They stand on a large mound overlooking the River Nith, just south of Drumlanrig Castle, the epitome of opulence from a later era. Tibbers is said to come from 'Tiberius Caesar', the original fort supposedly founded in Roman times. The stone remains date from a castle built in 1298 by Edward of England. The castle was later demolished by Bruce after Bannockburn, and was never rebuilt. The site is quite difficult to spot, its mound being covered by trees, but a signpost has been placed at the nearest farm gate, and a path leads eastwards over fields. The well in the middle of the ruins which was excavated in 1800, is carved through solid rock.

The Greyfriars monastery in Dumfries where Comyn's murder took place has long gone, but the name lives on in the Greyfriars Church in the town centre, which was built in 1866-67. This church stands on the site of the castle of Dumfries. An earlier church built in 1727 previously stood on the site, and some of the stonework of the castle was used in its construction. (MAP C21)

In front of the Greyfriars Church stands a statue of the poet, Robert Burns, who is buried in Dumfries. Burns wrote the words of *Scots Wha Hae* in Dumfries to the tune believed to have been the marching song of Bruce's troops, and Burns's words are a supposed rendering of the address Bruce gave to his men before the Battle of Bannockburn.

A few yards west of this statue towards the River Nith, a plaque has been inserted into the partition wall between two shops. The inscription runs:

Here stood the monastery
Of the Grey Friars where
on Thursday 10th February
1306 Robert the Bruce
aided by
Sir Roger Kirkpatrick
slew The Red Comyn and
opened the final stage

of the war for
Scottish Independence
which ended victoriously on
the Field of Bannockburn
1314
'I mak siccar'

The plaque was erected by the citizens
of Dumfries and the Saltire Society, and
marks as closely as possible the site of the
altar where Bruce and Kirkpatrick slew
Comyn. The plaque has as its top-piece a

Plaque in Dumfries

Lion Rampant shield surmounted by the crown of Scotland.

After the murder of Comyn, Bruce's men immediately ran into
the castle of Dumfries, and claimed it as the first to be taken for
Robert the First of Scotland. Although the murder of Comyn
would not seem to have been premeditated, Bruce would have
realised at once that there was no way back, and that he must
assume the crown and face what the future held. He had probably
hoped to wait until Edward was dead, but the die had been cast.

Christopher Seton, who had slain Comyn's uncle, was captured at Loch Doon Castle shortly after the murder, and was
brought back to Dumfries by Edward. He was drawn, hung and
beheaded on what is known locally as the Crystal Mount. His
widow, Bruce's sister, founded a chapel on the spot in his memory
and dedicated it to the Holy Rood which Edward had plundered
in 1296. The chapel was superseded by St Mary's Church, built
between 1837 and 1839.

Plans were drawn up to have Bruce crowned as quickly as
possible. He went to his family seat at Lochmaben to send out to
inform his supporters of the situation and spread the news of his
imminent coronation at Scone. He made his way north with his
retinue, heading for Glasgow, probably following the line of the
old Roman road up Annandale, which cuts over the hills into
Clydesdale and is still marked on OS maps. As the party started to

climb into the Lowther Hills, a few miles north of Moffat, a little south-west of the Devil's Beef Tub which was a favoured hiding place for stolen cattle from cross-border raids, a party of horsemen were spotted ahead, as if watching out for them from this view point.

The leader of the party was a slim, dark-haired, olive-skinned young man who introduced himself as James Douglas, the son of William, whom Bruce had delivered from the English several years before. The young man swore fealty to Bruce there and then, saying that he had not forgotten how Robert had saved his family from danger and that he wanted to become his true knight. This was the beginning of a relationship which was to end twenty-four years later in southern Spain.

Traditionally, Bruce and Douglas met at the Arrickstane, a name which survives today in Ericstone, a farm at the head of Annandale, and a hill above the Roman road. The Landranger OS map has a boulder named Ericstane to the south-west of the Devil's Beef Tub, but a thorough search of the hillsides has revealed that it has gone. There are a few scattered stones on the hills but nothing particularly noticeable. The view from above the A701 Moffat-Edinburgh road gives a huge panorama south over Annandale, with the hills of the Lake District in England visible on a clear day, so it would be an obvious spot to wait for riders from the south as they would be seen many miles distant. (MAP C35)

After Douglas had joined his party, Bruce made for Glasgow and a meeting with his friend, Bishop Wishart, at the Cathedral. The murder of Comyn had taken place in Wishart's diocese, but he absolved Bruce for the sin, before preaching to his congregation that fighting for Scotland's freedom was as important as taking part in a crusade. Wishart gave Bruce a Lion Rampant banner which he had tucked away in anticipation of better days, before riding north with him to Scone to preside at his coronation. Bishop Lamberton also came from Berwick to see his friend crowned.

The coronation took place at the Abbey Church of Scone, which unfortunately was swept away in 1559 by a mob fired up with religious zeal during the Reformation. It is one of the great losses of Scottish history. All that survives is the moot hill itself, the mound that stands opposite the later Scone Palace. The Stone of Destiny stood on top of this mound, and the king would sit upon it to be crowned, symbolising his relationship with the soil and rock of Scotland. The little chapel which stands on top of the moot hill is all that remains of a later parish church built in 1624. (MAP A8)

The Abbey at Scone appears to have stood where Scone Palace now stands. It was founded by Alexander I in 1114, and replaced an even older church dedicated to the Holy Trinity. The church supposedly stood by the little burial ground some 100 yards from the moot hill.

The village of Scone in medieval times was clustered about the Abbey. All that remains of the village today is the stone cross surrounded by trees by the old gateway to the Palace. Scone is now represented by the village of New Scone, two miles south-east of the moot hill.

Standing on top of the hill now it is difficult to picture how the scene must have appeared on Friday, 25 March 1306 at Bruce's coronation. This spot contains so much of the history of Scotland, so many crownings, so many ceremonies, and even a royal burial in the case of Robert II, that I feel something tangible should still exist in the air. But I do not get that feeling, the way I do at sites like Culloden or Flodden. Perhaps I need to go in the dead of winter, instead of on a summer's day like my last visit, to visualise Edward Longshanks' men running riot through the buildings, taking the Stone and looting the riches of this ancient capital of Caledonia. Perhaps then I could picture Bruce, the circlet of gold being lowered onto his brow, thoughts

The Moot Hill, Scone

racing through his head. Was he troubled by self-doubt as he realised the task ahead of him? Perhaps he was full of self-belief. Although the future held enough horror to destroy a hundred lesser men, he was never shaken from his course. He was made of stern stuff, the sort of man that others would risk all for.

Traditionally, the kings of Scots were enthroned by the Earl of Fife, who claimed the honour by being the senior Earl of Scotland. Fife, however, was in the pocket of Edward of England. Fife's aunt, Isabel, knew where her duty to her country lay, and she came to represent the Earldom and place Bruce on the throne of Scotland, even though she was the wife of the Earl of Buchan, Bruce's sworn enemy. At a later date, Isabel, Countess of Buchan, was to pay dearly for her patriotism at the hands of Edward of England.

It is believed that the gold circlet that was placed on Bruce's head is now incorporated in the Crown of Scotland which is on show at Edinburgh Castle among the other Honours of Scotland.

The ceremony was attended by several of the Earls of Scotland and by many from the lairds class. It was watched over by high-ranking churchmen, including David, the Bishop of Moray. Moray was later to provide much of the manpower dedicated to Bruce and Scotland's cause. Maurice, Abbot of Inchaffray, was also in attendance, and his services were soon to be called for.

Bruce's wife, Elizabeth, was of course regarded as Queen. It is not known if there was some ceremony for her advancement to royal status, but we can probably assume so. Apart from Bruce's love for Elizabeth in asking for her hand in marriage, he may have considered that she had qualities fit for a queen, knowing that he hoped one day to be king.

The coronation would have been a joyous affair, the monks at Scone doing their utmost to entertain the guests lavishly, but in spite of the light-heartedness of the occasion, every one of the Scots attending would be very aware of the shadow cast upon the scene by King Edward of England. It would not be long before he did his best to spoil the party.

CHAPTER 5

King Hob

KING EDWARD HEARD OF Bruce's kingship with incredulity. At first he refused to believe the reports coming from north of the border.

Meanwhile, Bishop Wishart used timbers meant for the repair of his cathedral at Glasgow to make siege engines to attack the English held castle at Kirkintilloch. Records of the Kirkintilloch area from the 1830s say that not a trace of the castle existed even then, although there are various earthworks in the area from Roman times. Wishart then went on to take the castle of Cupar in Fife, and although this is also long gone, it stood on the site known as School Hill.

On 5 April 1306, Edward appointed Aymer de Valence as his lieutenant in Scotland, giving him the power to 'raise dragon'. This meant the unfurling of the dragon banner which showed that no quarter would be given. De Valence was a cousin of Edward as well as brother-in-law of the murdered Comyn, so he would have a personal desire to destroy Bruce.

He captured Bishop Lamberton at Scotlandwell in Kinross, and moved on to Cupar where he captured Wishart. They were sent south in irons. (Bishop Wishart was never to see his beloved Scotland again. He was ransomed for release after Bannockburn, but by that time was blind.) De Valence then camped his men inside the walls of Perth. Perth was a strongly walled town, and the buildings huddled round St John's Church – hence St Johnstown of Perth, the name surviving in the town's football team.

On 18 June, Bruce approached Perth and challenged Valence to surrender the town or come out and fight. De Valence replied that the day being a Sunday, he would be happy to comply the next day. Bruce took him at his word, and retired a few miles west to Methven to bivouac for the night. The Scots camped on the low lying ground in woodland just east of Methven Castle, and were preparing the evening meal when English horsemen suddenly burst upon them through the trees. (MAP A7) Some Scots managed to grasp their weapons and mount their horses, but it was a piecemeal retaliation, and Methven turned into a rout. One chronicler reported that Bruce only managed to escape because he was not wearing an emblazoned surcoat but a plain one. Many Scots knights were captured, amongst them Bruce's nephew, Thomas Randolph. Sixteen gentlemen were executed later at Newcastle. One of these was the hereditary standard bearer of Scotland, Alexander Scrymgeour, who would have been carrying the Lion Rampant banner. There were some notable survivors though. David Murray, the Bishop of Moray, had escaped and fled to Orkney.

The four-square Castle at Methven, which is now a private residence, occupies the same site as the original, the present building

Methven Castle

having been constructed by Ludovic of Lennox at the time of James VI. The rout took place on the low lying ground just east of the Castle, north of the modern A85 road which runs between Perth and the village of Methven.

The survivors made their way west, passing the Abbey of Inchaffray, where Abbot Maurice helped their escape. Inchaffray in the Gaelic is *Innes-abh-reidh*, the island of the smooth water, and the abbey site was probably once surrounded by wet marshy ground, making it appear an island. The Abbey was founded in 1200 by the Earl of Strathearn. Parts of the walls were standing until 1816 when a road was built through the ruins. All that remains is a gable wall and a small vaulted chamber and pieces of scattered stonework. These lie in the garden of a private house, a mile or so south of the A85 about six miles east of Crieff.

Inchaffray Abbey

In order to take some photographs of the gable wall, I parked my motorcycle at the side of the road. I always ask for permission to enter someone's garden or ground to examine remains, and most people are only too happy to help. In this case the owner of the house came out to have a look at the bike, as he was a bit of a biker himself, and invited me on to his property for a look.

I knew that when the road had been built in 1816, several artefacts, many graves, and a small ivory cross were uncovered. The owner of the property now on the site told me how he had found the hilt of a sword in his garden, and hidden in stonework a leather pouch which had crumbled but had contained some old documents which had survived.

From Inchaffray Abbot Maurice guided Bruce and his followers west along Loch Earn side, turning north into Glen Ogle, and dropping into Glen Dochart. Maurice of Inchaffray was another churchman who was steadfast in the cause of Scottish independence. He was regarded as one of Bruce's most trusted advisers.

Bruce and his sadly depleted band found shelter in Glen Dochart from the pursuing English troops. Bruce visited the shrine of St Fillan, the remains of which can still be seen between Crianlarich and Tyndrum in Strathfillan. He perhaps had doubts after what had happened to so many of his friends and supporters at Methven, but the holy men gave him their blessing which obviously meant much to him, as several later charters and grants to the shrine testify.

The square-shaped bell of St Fillan, made of cast bronze with a double-headed dragonesque handle, lay on a gravestone from ancient times until it was stolen by an English traveller in 1798. It was restored to Scotland in 1869 and is now in the Museum of Scotland in Edinburgh, where the silver head of the crozier of St Fillan, another relic of Bruce's time, is also kept.

News of Methven and that Bruce was taking refuge in the Glen Dochart area did not take long to reach the ears of his enemies. John of Lorne, whose mother was an aunt of the Red Comyn, came upon Bruce's party, and Bruce's men had to fight a sharp rearguard action in order to escape. The place where this happened is commemorated today in the name of a farmhouse in Strathfillan called Dalry. This is the Gaelic *Dail-Righ*, or King's Field, obviously a legacy of the fight. (MAP C5)

The farm stands two miles south of Tyndrum, just west of the A82. The remains of the chapel of St Fillan are a little south-east of this, between the road and the River Fillan.

There is a tale that Bruce was set upon by three of John McDougall of Lorne's men, whereupon he drew his battleaxe and dispatched all three with great ferocity. One of his victims, falling backwards, managed to grasp the brooch on Bruce's tunic and it came away in his hand. This brooch, known to history as the

Brooch of Lorne, was handed down through generations of McDougalls, and although there has been some debate as to its authenticity, the McDougalls of Dunollie still have it in their possession. It contains a large crystal surrounded by eight pearls. The centre section unscrews and presumably held a relic or memento of some sort.

The Brooch of Lorne

After the escape from Dalry, Bruce knew that he would have to split his party up. His womenfolk had accompanied him and he had to get them to safety, so that with a few trusted companions, he could take to the heather and try to reach friendly territory where he could muster his followers.

Barbour, who wrote an epic poem about the life and deeds of Bruce later in the 14th century, mentions how Douglas was the great provider during these days of hardship, proving to be an excellent hunter. He was one of the small party that was to remain with Bruce. The others were dispersed, and a group of Bruce's gentlemen went north-east with the ladies to seek safety in Kildrummy Castle in Aberdeenshire. (MAP A1)

The imposing ruins of Kildrummy stand a couple of miles south-west of the village of Kildrummy, some ten miles north-west of the town of Alford. The castle started as a tower in the time of

Kildrummy Castle

Alexander II, but the ruins cover an area of an acre, with out-works covering two more, on top of a rocky eminence bordered by two ravines. The remains of a chapel stand within the castle ruins.

The fugitives reached Kildrummy and sanctuary, but their safety was short lived. Getting word of their flight, Aymer de Valence, together with the Prince of Wales, laid siege to Kildrummy, a traitor inside the castle setting fire to the stores, forcing the garrison to yield. The ladies, accompanied by the Earl of Atholl, managed to escape and headed north, probably hoping to reach Orkney.

Among those taken prisoner was Bruce's brother, Nigel, who was taken to Berwick where he was hung, drawn and beheaded. A similar horrific death was meted out to Sir Simon Fraser, who had been a loyal friend to Wallace, and had subsequently joined

Bruce's following. Fraser was hung, drawn and beheaded in London, and his head was set up on London Bridge alongside the head of Wallace. Edward was determined to subjugate Scotland – old age had not mellowed him, his hatred for Bruce on a par with the hatred he had felt for Wallace, still palpable today.

The ladies, with Atholl, had to cross the territory of William, Earl of Ross, who was still loyal to the cause of the absent John Balliol. He must have shown some aggression towards Bruce's kin, and they took refuge in St Duthac's Sanctuary in Tain in Easter Ross, seeking asylum. William of Ross violated the Sanctuary and handed his captives over to Edward's English troops. (MAP A6)

Bruce's influence was very much on the wane after his defeats at Methven and Dalry, and William, Earl of Ross, was obviously influenced by this, but it does not lessen my embarrassment at sharing his surname. His son, however, was to prove a stalwart in the cause for independence.

Tain was the supposed birthplace of Saint Duthac who was born about the year 1000. He died in Armagh in Ireland in 1065 and his remains were taken back to Tain in 1253, after which it became a shrine and noted sanctuary. Nearly every monarch of Scotland went there on pilgrimage, James IV going every year. A rough footpath across the nearby moor which still bears the name, the Kings' Causeway, was the traditional pilgrimage route. Scant ruins of the Sanctuary survive, and in the late 1800s were surrounded by a parapet wall and railing. The Sanctuary stood on a little knoll by the golf links.

St Duthac's, Tain

The church of St Duthac or Duthas in Tain was founded around 1360, and some ruins nearby are said to be the remains of a church of Culdee origin.

Another huge stain on the character of Edward of England is the way he took retribution on the female relatives and followers of Bruce and their accompanying menfolk. Although gruesome deaths were meted out to Scottish males who fell into Edward's clutches, the rules of chivalry laid down how women were to be regarded. But Edward's spleen cast all decency aside. Elizabeth, Bruce's wife, was confined in the Manor House of Burstwick in Holderness, to have contact with no-one save the two elderly women who served her meals. Edward was probably only lenient towards her because she was the daughter of his old friend, Richard De Burgh. Bruce's sister, Christian, the widow of Christopher Seton who had been executed at Dumfries, was confined in the nunnery of Sixhills in Lincolnshire. Worse was to befall Mary, Bruce's other sister, and Countess Isabel of Buchan, who had enthroned Bruce at Scone. They were confined in cages for all to gaze upon like animals, Mary at Roxburgh and Isabel at Berwick. They were allowed no communication or contact with anyone and were left in this barbaric state for several years. It was only after Bannockburn that Bruce was able to hand over high-ranking prisoners in order to secure their release.

Even more shocking was that Edward commanded Bruce's twelve-year-old daughter Marjorie to be locked in a similar cage mounted on a tower in the Tower of London. Fortunately, this order was soon revoked, and she was confined in a nunnery at Watton in Yorkshire.

The Earl of Athol, captured trying to defend the ladies, was a distant relative of King Edward. Edward commanded that he should be hung from an exceptionally high gallows. After his death, he was beheaded and his body burned.

Because of the sorry state of Bruce's campaign, he was referred to by Englishmen in a derogatory fashion as King Hob. He is even given this name on documents that have survived.

How would Bruce have felt when the tidings reached him of the executions that resulted from Methven, and the murder of his brother and the caging of his womenfolk? He must have been crippled with doubts, wondering what he had started, thinking of the pain his loved ones were enduring. His resolve and strength of character shone through. He knew that a king could not behave as an individual nor lie down in the face of adversity, but must put his nation before personal grief, no matter how long the odds. Knowing that his options were few, he made his way south, heading for the Lennox at the southern end of Loch Lomond. Malcolm, Earl of Lennox, was a staunch supporter of the cause and the only chance for Bruce and the handful of followers that remained with him, now travelling on foot.

Every Scottish schoolboy knows (or should know) the legend of Bruce and the spider, and there are several caves, scattered the length and breadth of Scotland, where this incident is claimed to have taken place. It is said to have happened when Bruce's fortunes were at their lowest ebb, and a cave on Loch Lomond side is a likely spot. It stands some distance north of Rowardennan on the eastern shore of Loch Lomond, and is marked on the os maps as Rob Roy's Cave, and on some other maps as Rob Roy's Prison, a connection with another historical Scottish figure from a later date. (MAP C7)

The story of Bruce and the spider is that Bruce was lamenting his losses and defeats, and did not know whether to continue. As he was sitting sheltering in a cave, mulling this over, he noticed a spider trying again and again to reach the far wall to get an anchor for the web it was trying to build. He watched the determination of the little beast, and admired its ability to never give up, and when it finally succeeded in its task, he realised that if a spider could strive and win against all the odds, so could he. (This story would seem to be internationally known. Once when booking into accommodation in Paris, the concierge asked where I came from. I replied, 'Scotland', at which point he exclaimed, 'Robert de Bruce and ze Spider!' – the first thing that sprang to his mind when he thought of my country.)

(Another 'Spider's Cave' is to be found near Kirkpatrick, a few miles north of Gretna. Taking the Kirkpatrick-Fleming exit from the M74, the cave is signposted from the village. It is within the boundaries of a caravan park, and is reached by a purpose-built walkway, as the entrance is halfway up a cliff-face above the river. Access was originally gained from a hanging rope. That Bruce once used this refuge is possible, since the ground on

Bruce Cave, Kilpatrick-Fleming

which it lies belonged to one of his early supporters.) (MAP C24)

At the north end of Loch Lomond, Glen Falloch runs towards Crianlarich. A stone stands on the hillside to the west of the glen and is called Clach-nam-Breatann (Stone of the Britons). It is marked on most good scale maps of the area. It gained its name by marking the northern extent of the territories of the Strathclyde Britons whose base was Dumbarton (Dun-Breatann) on the Clyde. There is a local tradition that Bruce sheltered by this stone. It may be only legend, but it shows how Bruce's flight through this area has been remembered over the centuries. (MAP C6)

Barbour in his epic poem tells how the small party came down to the banks of Loch Lomond, and scoured them for some means of transport to take them across the water to safer shores. Douglas found a little sunken rowboat which he hauled ashore, and tipping out the water, reckoned to be safe enough to take two across at a time. Barbour says that Bruce regaled his men with classic chivalric tales to amuse them during this lengthy process.

Having safely cleared the obstacle of Loch Lomond, Bruce's men split up to hunt deer, hunger having made this a priority. Purely by chance, some of them met Malcolm, Earl of Lennox, and there was great rejoicing at this encounter. Malcolm having heard no news since Methven, had assumed that Bruce had perhaps been slain.

Malcolm was able to lead Bruce's men to the Clyde to meet up with Sir Neil Campbell who had a couple of galleys provisioned and ready. Neil Campbell was to be one of Bruce's most loyal followers, and this loyalty was repaid in kind by grants of land from a grateful King, forming the basis of the later Campbell power in Scotland.

Bruce decided to make for the Kintyre Peninsula and Dunaverty Castle, about five miles north-east of the Mull of Kintyre. Dunaverty was in the hands of Angus McDonald of the Isles, or Angus Og as he was more commonly known (Og being the Gaelic for young, therefore Young Angus). Angus Og and Bruce appear to have taken to each other at once, and Angus was another who remained loyal to Bruce till the end of his days.

Dunaverty Castle has long gone. Even in the 1800s it was stated that it had been so completely demolished that scarcely a vestige remained. It stood on a steep pyramid-shaped peninsula some 95ft high, with cliffs descending to the sea, and defended on the landward side by ramparts and a ditch. The site is about ten miles south of Campbeltown. It was built to command the narrow sea channel between Scotland and Ireland, and was the scene of many turbulent encounters and much bloodshed in Scotland's history. (MAP C8)

According to Barbour, Bruce's galleys were chased on the voyage to Dunaverty, so it was decided that lingering too long there would enable more of his enemies to gather and perhaps besiege them. Bruce probably only stayed at Dunaverty for three nights before sailing away.

No-one really knows where Bruce spent the winter of 1306-1307, but whether he wintered in Ireland, the Hebrides or Orkney, he made a vow that he would take the first steps on the road towards freedom for his people and regaining his kingdom. Edward's horrific vengeance on his family and friends would soon in its turn be avenged.

Cambuskenneth
Where the spoil of Bannockburn was amassed. Bruce's body rested here
before his burial at Dunfermline.

Turnberry Castle

Bruce's birthplace. A lighthouse now stands among the castle ruins.

Castle Urquhart

Taken by Bruce as his army made their way through the Great Glen.

Roxburgh Castle

Scant ruins are all that remain of the mighty fortress taken by James Douglas.

Field of Bannockburn
Old print showing the Borestone. This is where the rotunda stands today.

Edward I and II
Supposed likenesses of Bruce's two great protagonists.

CHAPTER 6

The Wind of Change

BRUCE'S WHEREABOUTS THROUGH THE winter of 1306-7 are a mystery which has been debated endlessly over the years. Tantalising fragments of knowledge exist, but we shall probably never know the truth. Barbour says that Bruce made for Rathlin, an island off the north-east coast of Ireland. He may well have done, but he would have been an easy target if he had spent the winter there, England having no lack of shipping for assault, quite apart from Bruce's enemies locally with longships at their command.

Rathlin looks an unlikely place for a hunted man and his followers to find sanctuary. Barbour would perhaps find it a logical place for Bruce to go after leaving Dunaverty Castle, but if Bruce was there, it must have been just a short visit, as he could easily have been blockaded. Bruce more likely headed north up the western seaboard of Scotland, perhaps going as far as Orkney. Some people say he went to Norway, but if he visited Bergen, there would surely be some record in Norse writings.

It is possible he spent at least a little time at Castle Tioram, the ancient seat of Clanranald, the ruins of which stand complete to the wallhead on a tidal islet in Loch Moidart. The castle was the property of Christina of Gamoran, who later supplied Bruce with men and galleys. The curtain walls date from Bruce's time, whereas the tower is slightly later. The first time I visited it was on a glorious summer's day, and I was amazed at the abun-

Castle Tioram

dance of oysters in the surrounding sandy shallows, everything a riot of blues, greens and purples that make the western seaboard of Scotland unique. (MAP C1)

My second visit was the ultimate contrast in darkness and driving rain, the sea crashing around the walls. I was unable to see the stonework of the castle till I was within a few feet of it. Despite the weather, I spent a reasonable night within the ruins, tucked up in a roofed corridor – even the ghosts of the castle's chequered history did not bother me. It saw much bloodshed over the centuries, and was finally burnt during the 1715 rising. The clan chief, a Jacobite, guessed that if the rising failed, the castle would fall into his enemies' hands, a thought he could not bear. So he set fire to it himself before he marched away. The rising did fail, of course, and he did not return, and the gaunt shell of Castle Tioram has stood as it was the day he left. It can be reached by taking a small side road which runs west from the A861, a little after Acharacle at the foot of Loch Shiel. At the road end the castle is visible across the bay.

Angus Og had fortified properties scattered across the west of Scotland and the Inner Hebrides which would have provided shelter for Bruce during this time. There are local tales that Bruce visited certain places, but there is no proof.

The first real news is in February 1307 when two of Bruce's brothers, Thomas and Alexander, made a landing at Loch Ryan in Galloway, supported by men from Kintyre and from Ireland. (MAP C14) Unfortunately, the landing met with disaster, and they were defeated by the McDoualls of Galloway – enemies of the Bruces. They were taken, with Alexander badly wounded, to Carlisle, where Edward of England had them horribly executed. The heads of Alexander and the other leaders were attached to the gates of Carlisle as warning. Thomas's head was mounted on a pole above the castle keep.

Carlisle Castle is open to the public. It has a bloody and cruel past, a place where punishment was often meted out to Scots prisoners. (MAP B6)

Carlisle Castle

Alexander had attended university at Cambridge where he was regarded as the greatest scholar of his day. How different Scotland during Bruce's reign might have been, had Alexander survived to exert his influence.

Meanwhile, Douglas and Boyd, a loyal follower of Bruce from the Kilmarnock area, made a raid on the Isle of Arran, where they captured an English supply train carrying provisions for the castle at Brodick. Bruce, too, crossed to Arran at about this time.

Barbour tells how Bruce landed on Arran, blowing his horn. Douglas recognised it, and he and Bruce were re-united. (MAP C10)

In the south-west of Arran, on the coast looking over towards Saddell on the Kintyre peninsula, is the King's Cave which is reputed to have sheltered Bruce. Other

Brodick Castle

caves in the vicinity have names such as King's Kitchen, King's Larder, and so on. (MAP C9)

I came across the following information in a book from the 1830s. The estate of Kilmichael in Glen Cloy near Brodick and a farm on the west of the island were granted by Bruce to a family by the name of Fullarton for services rendered during his stay on Arran. The book commented that the family still resided on their estate, the owner retaining his charter of ownership from Bruce dated 26 November 1307.

Bruce, Douglas and Boyd could not remain on Arran, so a man named Cuthbert was sent across to the mainland to see how the land lay and find out what people were saying. Cuthbert was instructed to light a fire near Turnberry Point if conditions seemed favourable for Bruce to cross with his followers.

Turnberry Castle, Bruce's birthplace, was in English hands, and Bruce would certainly have known this. But more importantly, Cuthbert found that the populace of Carrick were cowed by their English oppressors, and therefore unlikely to commit themselves to backing Bruce.

By a strange quirk of fate, there was a fire in the vicinity of Turnberry which was spotted from Arran. Thinking this was the signal, Bruce's party set sail. The spot where they embarked is reputedly the small settlement of Kingscross in south-east Arran which looks over the First of Clyde to Turnberry. (MAP CII)

On landing, the King's party was met by Cuthbert who had seen the fire and feared that they would have taken it for the signal. Bruce had to decide whether to continue or retreat. With encouragement from his brother Edward, Bruce made the decision to continue the fight for Scotland's independence. I can picture him on the rocky shore, his men watching him, as he balanced things in his mind. It must be all or nothing, and the decision that he made in the gloom of a February night was to change the history of Scotland.

Turnberry Castle, under the command of Henry Percy, one of England's greatest barons and soldiers, was impregnable. But the castle was not large enough for all the English soldiers and many of them had been billetted in nearby houses. Bruce's men attacked and made short work of them, and the ensuing bedlam struck terror into those inside the castle. The scene where this took place is now covered by Turnberry Golf Course, although the modern Turnberry village is probably on the site of an original habitation.

Bruce was aided by Christian of Carrick, a local noblewoman. She gave him supplies and a band of fighting men – and perhaps more. She was quickly named as Bruce's mistress, with some justification it seems, as the records reveal that two of his natural children were named Neil and Christian of Carrick.

Barbour tells us that Bruce was informed at this time of the failure of the Galloway expedition and the death of its leaders, including, of course, his brothers Thomas and Alexander. He probably also learned of the fate of Nigel and of his womenfolk and their caging in various castles.

Bruce was a man of some intellect, as well as being a commander of genius. He knew that the only way he could help his loved ones was to fight back hard and win, in order to gain their release and avenge the horrific and agonising deaths his brothers had suffered at the hands of Edward. He marched south towards the Galloway hills, ready for confrontation.

Barbour summed up Bruce's feelings at this time thus:

'And since yon Edward, England's king
Thinks Scotland is too small a thing
To share between himself and me
Then mine entirely shall it be!'

Edward had sent letters north to his various commanders, expressing his amazement that Bruce had not been captured. In April 1307, the English made a raid into Glen Trool to try and

Bruce Stone, Glen Trool

capture Bruce and were repulsed with heavy losses. Bruce had realised that he could never match the English in terms of manpower, so Scotland itself would have to make up for the deficit. His men used the rough country in Glen Trool, which cradles the lovely Loch Trool, to thwart and confuse the English troops, for instance rolling stones down the steep slopes at the enemy. (MAP C15)

The battle is said to have taken place on the ground at the head of the loch, and most maps place it there. From the A714 a road runs up one side of Glen Trool, and where this peters out in a series of parking places, it is only a few yards to the modern monument commemorating the battle. This is a large rectangular block standing on top of a cairn of boulders, on a knoll with a panoramic view over loch and glen.

Another commemoration of Bruce can be found in the area near Clatteringshaws Loch. As the crow flies it is not too far from Glen Trool, but by road one must go first to Newton Stewart, then take the A712 to New Galloway. Just by Clatteringshaws Loch a signposted path leads a few hundred

Bruce's Stone, Moss Raploch

yards into the forest to a boulder, perhaps 10ft in height and width, known as Bruce's Stone. A wooden signboard bears the message:

BRUCE'S STONE
Here on Moss Raploch, King Robert
the Bruce defeated an English army in 1307.
It is said that Bruce rested against this stone
after the battle.

This board was erected by the National Trust for Scotland. (MAP C18)

There is no official record of a battle at Moss Raploch, but that does not mean a skirmish of some sort did not take place there during the time Bruce spent with his men in the Galloway hills.

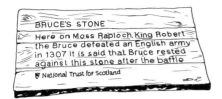

Sign at Moss Raploch

Also in this area are the remains of Kenmure Castle, John Balliol's supposed birthplace, only a few hundred yards south of New Galloway, between the A762 and the head of Loch Ken.

From Galloway Bruce struck north and met the English forces under Aymer de Valence in battle at Loudoun Hill near Darvel in Ayrshire. Loudoun Hill is an ancient fortified site which was used by local tribes before becoming a Roman fort. Wallace is said to have avenged his father's murder here by attacking and routing an English force.

It has been remarked that Loudoun Hill is possibly the best defensive site in all southern Scotland. (MAP C26) A volcanic plug standing 840ft high, its soaring crags are visible from many miles around. A farm road strikes off the A71 directly opposite the Loudounhill Inn, and goes up round the hill, giving easy access to the summit. A panoramic view is laid out, with Arran visible to the west and moorland stretching away to Strathaven in the east. The infant River Irvine runs directly below. The summit is obviously the best place to view the battlefield, but care should be taken if there has been rain. The grassy northern flank which offers the easiest ascent is notoriously slippy when wet. Local farmers have erected stiles over fences, and for those who cannot make it to the top, the farm road directly east of the hill has a car park and viewpoint.

Just underneath the trig point on the summit of the hill, a granite plaque has been inserted into the rocks. It commemorates Bruce's victory on 10 May 1307, stating that the plaque was carried here by willing hands, and celebrates Bruce 'freeing us from serfdom'. Some local Ayrshire lads apparently took the initiative and raised this small monument by their own

Plaque at Loudoun Hill

efforts. It appeared some time during the 1980s. It is kept clean and the paintwork is regularly renewed.

Bruce stationed his men astride the River Irvine, and the English came charging up the valley from the Darvel direction. Knowing the English would be mostly mounted, Bruce had pits dug in front of the Scottish line, and also used the terrain – there was a lot of bog in the area, the little bit of firm ground narrowing rapidly in front of his position.

As the English charged, their lines started to buckle, the riders on the flanks squeezing in to avoid the bog that threatened to make their horses flounder. In some disorder, they hit the first of the pits, which broke up their advance even more, and there were further pits ahead to be negotiated. As the English began to falter, Bruce's men charged forward, and the English knights tried to turn back. It soon became a rout, horses charging piecemeal back towards Darvel, the jubilant Scots in pursuit. Aymer de Valence fled for the safety of Bothwell Castle.

Three days later Bruce came upon a force of Englishmen under the Earl of Gloucester, and attacking at once, routed them too. They were forced to flee to the safety of Ayr and its English-held castle. Bruce continued his campaign in the south-west, becoming the terror of English garrisons.

The news of these victories would have spread like wildfire, from farm to farm across the country, the talk of the taverns in the towns and villages. Many who had lived their lives as best they could under an army of occupation, rose and went to join the freedom fighters who fought alongside Bruce, jubilant at the victories over the hated English. Edward had threatened to burn and hang any who opposed him in Scotland, but this had the opposite effect to that intended – many people were ready to join Bruce rather than suffer injustice under English law, and they flocked to his banner.

But the best piece of news for Scotland was not the news of any battle, but that Edward of England was dead. He was gone, and Scotland still existed as a nation. He died on 7 July 1307.

The last few months of his life were spent at Lanercost Priory near Brampton in Cumbria, just south of Hadrian's Wall. (MAP B7) He had based himself there to direct operations against Scotland. Hearing of Bruce's continuing success against his occupying forces, he decided to lead another invasion into Scotland in person, even though his health was beginning to fail. He reached Carlisle when he was forced to take to his sick bed. When more news of Bruce's victories came, he declared himself fit, donated his litter to Carlisle Cathedral, mounted his horse and marched north. The hatred in his heart willed him onwards, but as the English army reached the Solway shore, just north of Burgh-on-Sands, intending to cross the Solway Sands at low tide, he realised his end was near. (MAP B5)

He commanded his son, Edward, that after his death his body was to be boiled till the flesh left the bone. The flesh could be discarded, but his skeleton was to be carried before his army and was not to be laid to rest till the last Scot was crushed underfoot. Prince Edward was very different from his warlike father, and when Longshanks breathed his last, he had his body disembowelled and his brain removed in readiness for the long funeral procession south to Westminster Abbey in London.

(Removal of organs from the dead was very common in those days, and I am often asked why this was done. The answer is simple. It would sometimes take weeks to transport the dead to their last resting place. Roads were muddy tracks or practically non-existent, and the body would start to decay and smell after a few days. In the circumstances it made sense to remove entrails, if only for the sake of those who had to transport the body).

A stone pillar surrounded by iron railings marks the spot where Edward expired. Entering the village of Burgh-on-Sands from the Carlisle direction, a right turn just after the church leads to a parking place from which the monument is visible half a mile distant. From there a path leads the last few hundred yards to the monument. This is where a motorcycle comes into its own, as there is always a corner to tuck it into.

The view from the monument is the same as that which

Edward would have seen as he died, cursing Scotland to the last. You can imagine the huge army camped out on the grassland, standing idle as their king gave up the ghost.

Edward's brain and entrails were interred in the Abbey of Holm Cultram, which stands in the village of Abbeytown south-west of Carlisle. Holm Cultram seems to have been a favourite place of Longshanks, even though it was founded by Scots monks from Melrose Abbey. There is no memorial to him there, but it is odd to walk around this ancient building, knowing that the brain which spewed out so much evil towards the people of Scotland lies somewhere within its walls.

Lanercost Priory is not far from Holm Coltram. It is some ten miles east of Carlisle, just outside the village of Brampton. Lanercost is a jewel, part of it still used for worship. It stands in a lovely valley through which runs the River Irthing. Both Wallace and Bruce visited it, and shortly before his death, Edward had stayed in the building known as the 'guest house' which is inhabited to this day.

Edward's tomb in Westminster Abbey is a large unadorned sarcophagus which lies in the chapel of Edward the Confessor. Inscribed on one side are the words:

Edwardus Primus, Malletus Scotorum Rex, Pactum Serva
(or, Edward the First, Hammer of the Scots, Keep Faith.)

Hammer of the Scots may have been the title Edward used. He rode over the land, but never reigned over it. All he succeeded in doing was creating enmity between two nations that had been reasonably good neighbours. Perhaps his most fitting epitaph is that the people of Scotland still abhor his memory.

CHAPTER 7

Consolidation

AFTER EDWARD'S DEATH IN 1307, Bruce must have realised that there was light at the far end of the tunnel, still a distance away, but discernable. He spent the remaining months of that year consolidating his rule over a united Scotland, and with the immediate English threat somewhat diminished, he could deal with the Comyn and Balliol sympathisers.

Edward II entered Scotland after his father's death, marching his army as far as Cumnock before retiring homewards without achieving anything of consequence.

Bruce decided to march north, but he left Douglas in the south to counter any threat that might arise. Douglas was still only about twenty, but Bruce must already have been struck by his personality and ability which led people ever after to remember him as one of the most loyal and brilliant soldiers Scotland produced.

Douglas made his way to his homeland of Douglasdale in Lanarkshire, determined to free his inheritance from the invaders. Douglas Castle, the subject of Sir Walter Scott's *Castle Dangerous*, was a place of strength, so some subterfuge was required to capture it. Douglas called on a local, Thomas Dickson, and asked for his advice. Dickson knew that the garrison would attend mass at the nearby St Bride's church to celebrate Palm Sunday, so it was agreed that this would be the best opportunity to strike. (MAP C27)

Douglas's supporters mingled with the English once they were within the church, arms hidden beneath their everyday clothes. At a given signal, they turned on the English, and a fierce fight ensued, the Scots gradually gaining the upper hand. The fight won, a group of Scots raced to the castle, to find it had been left in charge of only two men, the porter and the cook who was preparing the Sunday dinner. The Scots took charge, and one of the foremost strongholds of the country was now in their hands.

Douglas was determined that a good meal should not go to waste, and his men sat down to dinner. Once they had eaten their fill, Douglas had all the castle's provisions opened and scattered in the cellar. The English who had survived the fight were executed, and their bodies were added to the mess. Douglas smashed open all the barrels of wine. The castle was then fired, and the people took to the nearby hills and dales to avoid reprisals.

St. Brides, Douglas

This carnage was later to be called ironically The Douglas Larder. There used to be a restaurant in East Kilbride named The Douglas Larder, and it brought a smile to my face to think of diners munching away, most of them oblivious to the story behind the name.

The Douglas Castle site is marked by the gaunt remains of one round tower, standing in parkland east of the village of Douglas, a couple of miles west of the M74 motorway in southern Lanarkshire.

Driving through the village, the little church of St Bride's stands on top of a knoll. The aisle is all that remains of the original church where the locals turned on the English garrison. A sign at the graveyard gate gives the name of the keyholder in the village who will hand over

Douglas Castle

the key to the church. Douglas himself rests for eternity within the church, but that will be covered later.

Looking from the door of the church you will see a stream which wends its way through the valley. This is the Douglas Water – from which Douglas and Douglasdale take their name. In the Gaelic it is *Dubh Glas* (pronounced Doo-Glas, which is how the name of the village is pronounced locally); this means the black water, and the peaty stream is the origin of the name Douglas. There are fifty-six towns and villages in the world with the name Douglas, which shows how the sons and daughters of this village have scattered over the face of the planet.

Standing at the church door, you can see an old building over to the left. This is the museum, open from mid-afternoon at week-ends and run by enthusiastic locals, which deals with enquiries from Douglases from all over the world.

The entrance to the castle policies lies a little east of St Bride's church. You can park and walk the several hundred yards to the castle site, passing the loch with its swans. (It is wise to carry something to give them to eat, as they will follow the length of the loch, hoping for a tit-bit.) The raised ground has been the site of several variants of Douglas Castle. The later mansion of the Douglas family was demolished in the 1930s, but photographs of it can be seen in the museum. The surviving gatehouse of the mansion, with the Douglas coats of arms, is in the grounds of Happendon Services on the M74.

This area, with its trees, stream, hill and moor, coupled with its part in the history of Scotland, has always been magical to me. I love to wander down to the bridge over the Douglas and peer into its murky sluggish depths as James Douglas must have done on many occasions. If he were here today, he would still recognise this landscape as his own.

Further west up Douglasdale stands a house called Hazelside. This is the site of the farm belonging to Thomas Dickson who advised Douglas about the movements of the English garrison. It still belonged to his descendents in the 17th century. Dickson became a loyal follower of Bruce, and served with Douglas. Bruce later granted him the lands of Symington in Lanarkshire in gratitude for his services. Hazelbank is a large private house, but it can be seen from near where a minor road branches off the A70 towards Crawfordjohn.

While Douglas and his men struck east and south, becoming the scourge of Englishmen in that part of Scotland, Bruce led his small army north to counter his enemies there, and to let himself be seen in other parts of his kingdom. In October he arrived in Lochaber, and managed to take Inverlochy Castle, a power base of the Comyn family. (MAP C2)

The remains of the castle stand on the side of the River Lochy just north of Fort William. (It should not to be confused with the baronial hotel of the same name.) The castle is square, with a

Inverlochy Castle

round tower at each corner, and had been built by the Comyns around 1275. There was a bloody battle here between Montrose and the Campbells in 1645.

Fort William was known as Inverlochy until the erection of a fort in the area, built by the London government for the pacification of the Highlands, and the name of the town was then changed to Fort William.

Bruce moved up the Great Glen, destroying Castle Urquhart on Loch Ness, (MAP A5) razing Inverness Castle and burning Nairn. Bruce realised that for the English to control Scotland, they had to garrison the castles to subdue the local populations. No castles meant nowhere to garrison and nowhere to sleep safely at night.

Every castle Bruce and his men took, they destroyed or at least made uninhabitable. Orders were issued for every fortress to be made useless to the invaders.

Bruce's enemies in the north took fright, realising there was little to stop the growing momentum of Bruce's campaign. He was sweeping eastwards when suddenly he was struck by a serious illness. This was a major blow. The strain of life was taking its toll. Bruce had had the fate of so many of his followers to cope with, coupled with constant compaigning, living with the threat of conflict and attack, and more often than not sleeping under the stars, that his defences had eventually broken down through sheer exhaustion. His men formed a human cordon about him.

The Earl of Buchan, the Red Comyn's uncle, saw his chance. Mustering a respectable force, he attacked Bruce's men who were positioned at Slioch. This stands a little to the east of Huntly, just north of the A96 road. Legend states that Bruce's troops occupied Robin's Height and Meet Hillock. Bruce had probably started to enlist the help of the men of Moray, who were always stalwarts where Scotland's freedom was concerned. When Buchan's men arrived, on Christmas Day 1307, they found Bruce's men ranked in good order, looking fierce and warlike, and all that happened was some bickering between the two forces, and the exchange of a few arrows and spears. (MAP A2)

Luckily, Bruce's health returned, and he retired a little westwards to destroy various castles in enemy hands. Advancing east again during May 1308, it was only a matter of time before things came to a head between his forces and those of the Earl of Buchan.

The crunch came on the road between Inverurie and Old Meldrum, north-west of Aberdeen. Bruce's men based themselves at Inverurie, while Buchan's were at Old Meldrum. Buchan's force, some 1,000 strong, advanced on Bruce's 700 or so, and Bruce's men came towards them in good order. It turned into a running fight, Buchan's men retreating back towards Old Meldrum, panic taking hold. It soon became a rout. As it was a running fight, there is no particular battle site, but the B9170 is probably the line of much of the action, most likely in the area at Barra Castle, under Barra Hill. The fight in Barbour's narrative is called the Battle of Old Meldrum, but I have also seen it named Inverurie. Barra Hill has a prehistoric fort on its summit which locals used to point out as 'Comyn's Camp'. Modern maps still name an old fort a little south-east of Inverurie 'Bruce's Camp', but although this is only a local tale, it depicts the directions from which the two armies approached. (MAP A4)

There are no monuments to the battle, but the Battle of Harlaw, which was fought a couple of miles west of this in 1411, is marked by a large tower.

This area is part of the old parish of Bourtie, and the parish church, rebuilt in 1806, stands in Kirkton of Bourtie, one mile south of Barra Hill and two miles south of Old Meldrum, on a little farm road. An article, written in the 1890s, that I came across in an old gazetteer intrigued me. It stated:

> Two rude stone statues of a mailed knight and a lady, lying in the churchyard, are currently held to be those of a Sir Thomas and Lady de Longueville. He, runs the story, was Bruce's brave English comrade, who, wounded to death in the battle, shot an arrow hither from the dykes of Fala, to mark the spot where he would lie, and she, his dame, died when the tidings reached her.

I journeyed north to have a look. There are some interesting ancient standing stones in the area, old even in Bruce's time, but of these tombs in the churchyard I could find no trace. (The only peculiarity was a hedgehog which had been awakened prematurely from hibernation by a recent visit from grass-cutters. I buried him in a pile of leaves under a bush, but that was the only burial place I was involved in that day.) The thought occurred to me that the tombs might have been moved inside the church for safe-keeping, but the doors were locked and I was unable to gain access.

The Earl of Buchan's power was now broken, and he fled south.

But Bruce had to teach his opponents a lesson and he exacted a retribution that would strike fear into them, and have them examining their positions. His enemies in the north-east were put to the sword, farms were burned and cattle were slaughtered. Barbour mentions that fifty years later, men still mourned the 'Hership (Harrying) of Buchan'.

The Earl of Ross, who had handed Bruce's ladies over to Edward, now realised his coat was on a very shaky nail, and he submitted himself to Bruce at the Castle of Auldearn near Nairn. Bruce showed magnanimity towards his enemies, if they were willing to yield, and this was unparalleled for the times. Although it must have galled him to accept the peace of people who had been responsible for so much heartache, he looked at the situation from a monarch's point of view, putting his personal feelings aside and the good of Scotland to the fore.

His next move was to deal with the McDoualls in Galloway who had sent Bruce's brothers, Thomas and Alexander, to their hideous end at Carlisle. For this campaign, Bruce sent his surviving brother, Edward, with a body of troops in summer 1308 to batter any resistance in Galloway into submission. Edward was a renowned fighter, although he lacked the fine judgement of his elder brother. An expedition into the fastnesses of Galloway was more than likely right up his street. Bruce showed foresight by offering Edward the Lordship of Galloway once the task had been completed. Edward would naturally have been happy to crush any opposition, but would take care not to destroy too much of what might be his future property.

The details of the campaign are lost to us, but one battle was fought near Buittle, a castle on the water of Urr near Dalbeatie. Barbour places this battle on the Cree, but Professor Barrow, in his work on Bruce, points to it having taken place more likely on the Dee. Little remains of Buittle today, because, like so much else, it was destroyed when it was eventually captured by Bruce sometime in 1313. (Confusingly, there is a later tower-house in the area, also named Buittle.)

Barbour wrote:

But he with fewer followers met them
Near the Cree (?) and there beset them
Fiercely, in a stalwart fight
And quickly put them all to flight
And slew at least two hundred men
Their leaders fled for refuge then
To Buittle where they thought to be
Well cared for, and from danger free.

Barbour goes on to tell how Edward Bruce defeated 1,500 with 50. Edward and his followers came across the trail of a large body of men very early on a misty morning. They followed the trail, and when the mist lifted, their foes were only a bowshot away. Edward immediately charged, cutting through the enemy, then turned to cut through once more. As they turned for a third charge, their foes, disorientated, panicked and broke.

Barbour says that he was told what happened by Sir Alan Cathcart who was a member of Edward Bruce's party. It is therefore an eye-witness account.

Edward did not have the engines or man-power needed to reduce the castles of Galloway immediately. They would be taken at various times between the end of this campaign and Bannockburn in 1314.

During August 1308, Bruce made a foray into the lands of his enemies in Argyll, the MacDougalls. On this occasion, he was accompanied by James Douglas. The MacDougall power was based around Loch Awe, with their main seat at the ancient castle of Dunstaffnage which stands just north of the A85 between Oban and Connel. It was once home to the fabled Stone of Destiny.

As Bruce and his men made their way west down Glen Lochy towards Dalmally, following the track which has been superceded by the A85, Bruce must have been very aware that the MacDougalls would try to attack him somewhere en route. When they reached Loch Awe and his guides pointed out the deep defile of the Pass of Brander, Bruce realised that they would probably be attacked there. After all, it was the spot he would have chosen if the roles were reversed. (MAP C4)

Bruce had been actively campaigning for too long to be ambushed easily. He sent Douglas with a party of highlanders up and over the shoulder of Ben Cruachan, most likely hidden by darkness or early morning mist. Cruachan (3,689ft) stands north of Brander, and it is the mountain's steep flanks falling directly to Loch Awe that make the pass such a formidable place. Even today, travelling by road or rail through the pass, you cannot help but be struck by the lack of room for maneouvre, and the appropriateness of the spot for attacking any unwelcome visitors.

Douglas and his men got themselves into position above the pass, most likely having crossed where the Cruachan Dam now stands in a corrie. I have walked extensively in this area, doing a bit of 'Munro Bagging', and am familiar with the ground Douglas's men would have traversed. Down below, Bruce advanced steadily through the pass, till he came across the front line of MacDougall's defenders. He attacked at once, and Douglas's men, hearing the noise, attacked from above with boulders and arrows, before charging down, swords drawn.

The MacDougalls, finding themselves attacked from two sides, fled to cross the River Awe which flows from the far side of the pass, hoping to destroy the bridge there and thwart Bruce's advance. But Bruce's men chased them with such speed that they were unable to destroy the bridge and were at Bruce's mercy. He pushed forward and captured Dunstaffnage.

While he was in the area, Bruce is said to have held a parliament at St Modan's, or as it is more commonly known, Ardchattan Priory. It is said that this was the last parliament of Scotland where Gaelic was the language spoken. But it is known that Bruce held his first parliament at St Andrews on 16 and 17 March 1309. Some sort of council must have taken place at Ardchattan to decide events after the fight at Brander, and this has been misinterpreted as a parliament. A few ruins are all that remain of Ardchattan which stands north-east of Connel, on the shores of Loch Etive. (MAP C3)

Meanwhile, in the south James Douglas was near Peebles with his men. They were on a foray and were approaching a cottage which stood near the Water of Lyne which flows into the Tweed a few miles west of Peebles in the Happrew area. The Water of Lyne flows alongside the A72. Wallace fought one of his final fights in this vicinity. (MAP B10)

Douglas and his men heard voices within the cottage, and surrounding it, burst through the door. Inside was a group of Englishmen and with them was Thomas Randolph, Bruce's nephew. He had been captured after Bruce's defeat at Methven, and rather than languish in an English dungeon, he had agreed to fight for England. This was fairly common practice during those times. He appeared to have been indoctrinated with English ideals, had heard the tales of King Hob, and was of the opinion that Bruce was not a man of chivalry in a chivalric age – he had been told that Bruce relied on hit-and-run tactics, using the terrain, whereas if he were a real knight, he would face the might of England in an open field of battle.

Douglas took Randolph to Bruce, who was ready to accept him with open arms, but Randolph accused him of cowardice. Bruce had Randolph placed under close arrest until his manners improved. It did not take long for Randolph to grasp the reality of the situation, that the Scots were outnumbered ten to one by their aggressors, and Bruce's methods prevented much bloodshed amongst his own countrymen. Bruce's magnetism obviously played its part too, and it was not long before Randolph became one of his most trusted commanders, so much so, that in later years, after Bruce's death, he would become Guardian of Scotland.

CHAPTER 8

The Castles Recaptured

THE YEARS FROM THE TIME of the Brander episode and the Galloway campaigns until Bannockburn were spent retaking control of the castles from the invaders. There must have been some astonishing tales of acts of courage and daring, which have been lost in the mists of time, but Barbour and others have saved some of them for posterity. One is the story of William Binnie, who resided close to Linlithgow in West Lothian.

There had been a fortification of some sort on the mound jutting into Linlithgow Loch since the time of King David I. In 1301-2, Edward Longshanks commandeered the site to construct a peel – a stone building surrounded by a deep ditch and wooden palisade. The large garrison stationed there inflicted great harm on the local population, who must have been greatly cheered by the exploits of Bruce – so much so that William Binnie formulated a plan to rid them of the English who had been such a thorn in their flesh. Binnie had to take supplies of hay into the peel for the garrison, and he confided his ideas to some friends.

Eight of them concealed themselves under the hay in his cart, and others hid near the entrance to the peel itself. As Binnie approached with his delivery of hay, the porter, recognising him, opened the gate without any thought of danger. Binnie halted his cart within the gateposts so that they could not be closed. One of his companions cut the traces connecting the cart to the hauling oxen, while Binnie cleaved the porter's head with a blow, shouting 'Call all! Call all!', the signal to the men concealed in the hay and to those near the gates to rush forward to take the peel. All the English were slain, and the place was soon made secure. Various Englishmen who were absent from the garrison on sundry duties received a shock when they returned later in the day to find there had been a change of tenancy, and they had to flee to the castles at Edinburgh and Stirling which were still in English hands. (MAP A13)

Bruce was soon told of the situation and gave orders that the peel was to be utterly destroyed. Binnie was suitably rewarded for his services, and was granted land in the area. This grant survives in the names of a farm called West Binny, a property called Binny House and in Binny Craig or Crag, all situated a little north of Uphall. Binny Craig can be reached from the farm road which runs across its south side; a footpath crosses the fields, running between fences, leading to its base. It is another of those strange geological features, no doubt the remains of an ancient volcano, similar to Loudoun Hill and Edinburgh Castle Rock, which has a slope at one side, terminating in a sheer drop. It is a magnificent viewpoint, as are Cairnpapple Hill, with its ancient burial cairns, and Cockleroy Hill, whose summit Wallace used as a viewpoint, both a couple of miles west of Binny Craig. All three are excellent vantage points in this lovely and little-known corner of Scotland between the M8 and M9 motorways.

A family by the name of Binning in Lothian claim descent from the Binnie of Bruce's day, and have as their coat of arms a haywain with the motto 'Virtute doloque' (By strenth and guile).

Linlithgow Palace was the birthplace of James V and Mary Queen of Scots. It was obviously a building of great beauty when at the height of its power. All of this was lost when it was burnt in 1746 in a supposedly accidental fire started by the soldiers of the Butcher Cumberland. The shell that was left is mostly of buildings from the early 1400s.

Douglas's fame as a soldier was spreading far and wide. Amongst his followers was a man by the name of Sim of the Leadhouse which is in the vicinity of Crossford in the Clyde Valley. Sim devised a piece of equipment which was to prove invaluable to the Scots – the rope ladder. It was used during an attempt to capture the castle at Berwick. Unfortunately the barking of a dog alerted the guards and the Scots had to beat a hasty retreat, leaving their ladders behind. These were hauled in and displayed in Berwick, where they were seen by the author of a chronicle written at Lanercost Priory. The Lanercost Chronicle gives a very accurate description of the ladders, saying how they were made with slats of wooden steps between two ropes, which were suspended from an angled iron hook. The back of this hook had a ring protruding from it. The angled hook could be lifted up over a wallhead by inserting a spear tip into the ring and raising it into position. The ladders could easily be rolled up and carried behind a saddle.

Douglas had greater success with the ladders at Roxburgh. In order to get close to the walls to bring the ladders into use, Douglas devised a plan whereby his men covered themselves in black cloaks and crawled forward in single file to the castle walls. They were spotted by the guards on the wallhead, but in the dark they were assumed to be a line of straying cattle.

A ladder was hooked into place, but a member of the garrison came along the parapet to find out what the noise was. He reached the ladder just as Sim of the Leadhouse appeared at the top, and Sim was able to despatch him quickly with his dirk and tip his body over the wall. The rest of the party got their ladders in place and clambered up. The English were appalled to hear the dreaded cry of 'Douglas! Douglas!' within the town walls, and were soon overrun. The English governor, however, managed to lock himself in the main tower, but he was badly injured by an arrow in the face and agreed to surrender if Douglas would let him and his men return to England. This was agreed, and Roxburgh's towers and walls tumbled to the ground.

The site and scant remains of Roxburgh Castle stand just above the junction of the Rivers Tweed and Teviot, near Kelso. There is a long mound with fragments of walling dating from 1378, and it is still possible to trace the line of the moat. Roxburgh with its castle was one of the most important towns of Scotland, and it is strange that this is all that is left of a once busy centre of population. A later village of Roxburgh exists, but this stands a few miles south-west of the original site. The A699 road runs right under the castle remains, but parking can be difficult. (MAP B12)

The impressive mansion visible to the north from the castle mound is Floors Castle, home of the Duke of Roxburghe.

Another great story concerning the recapture of castles during this period is that of the fall of Edinburgh. Thomas Randolph, having taken an oath of fealty to Bruce, had become a trusted follower and was proving his worth as a level-headed soldier. He had been given the task of capturing Edinburgh, and it was proving to be a very difficult nut to crack. Douglas and Randolph had a friendly rivalry, each trying to outdo the other in feats of arms. When news of the fall of Roxburgh reached Randolph, and how it had been taken by a ruse, he mused on how Edinburgh Castle could be taken by a similar stratagem. By chance he met William Francis.

William Francis had stayed within the castle as a youth, and used to sneak out to visit a girl in the town. He told Randolph that he could lead a party unseen up the castle rock during the night, as he was sure he had not forgotten the route At the top a 12ft ladder would let them clear the wall. Francis lead the way on the appointed night, accompanied by Randolph and thirty men. (I remember climbing the castle rock to the wall during my teens, accompanied by a couple of friends. It could not have been that difficult as I was eating an ice-cream cone the whole way up – but that is not to say that I had chosen a route where I would not easily be noticed from above!) (MAP A15)

Barbour states:

The crag was high and hideous
The climbing was right perilous
If any chanced to slip or fall
He would be dashed to pieces all.

Before the last push to the top, they rested on a ledge beneath the wall. A guard came by, and they held their breath. If they were spotted, the garrison could easily finish them off by throwing rocks and stones down on them. There was a heart-stopping moment when a single stone came bouncing down, the guard calling out, 'Away, I see you clear!' There were a few seconds of silence, then the guard moved on. He had simply been amusing himself, or perhaps fooling a companion.

Randolph's men reached the wall, put up their ladder, and William Francis was first over, followed by Sir Andrew Gray, with Randolph next. Others followed. However, the guards spotted them, and a fierce fight ensued. It was a close run thing, but Randolph's men won, and another major fortress was back in the hands of its rightful owners.

Edinburgh Castle today is the most popular tourist attraction in Scotland. The main entrance is flanked by statues of Wallace and Bruce. (It is interesting that everybody seems to say 'Wallace and Bruce'. 'Bruce and Wallace' does not have the same ring to it, probably because Wallace came first chronologically.) Edinburgh Castle has changed hugely since the early 1300s. Bruce had the defences destroyed, so nothing exists from that era except St Margaret's Chapel on the highest point of the rock.

Bruce Statue, Edinburgh Castle

I find it quite poignant to visit certain buildings, knowing that they would be recognised by Bruce, Douglas or Randolph. It is as if some tangible presence has been left behind. It could never have occurred to them that 700 years on, someone like me would make a hobby out of

St Margaret's Chapel, Edinburgh Castle

visiting sites that had a connection with them, albeit on my very own steed, which has about 150 brake horse power!

Bruce was not to be outdone by his captains. While they were busy in the south, he was concentrating on ousting Englishmen north of the Forth and Clyde.

He had besieged the walled town of Perth for six weeks, and as on so many other occasions, he realised that a ruse of some sort would save time, effort and bloodshed. He made a close inspection of the walls, ditches and moats, then ordered his men to pack up all their gear and depart. The defenders of Perth, of course, took this opportunity to shout abuse and make gestures at Bruce's departing force. Bruce took his men west in the direction of Methven, where he had suffered his humiliating defeat a few years before.

They lay low for a week, letting the garrison in Perth be lulled into a false sense of security. Then, one dark night, Bruce put his plan into action. They came back to Perth under cover of darkness, and Bruce told his men that he had discovered a section of the moat where the water was no more than neck deep. He explained that they would cross, then use their scaling ladders to clear the walls. There was a French knight of some renown in Bruce's company, and he later reported his astonishment when Bruce suddenly pulled off his clothing and was the first to drop into the icy water and begin to wade across the moat. This was the root of Bruce's genius. Scots have always fought best when led by example and Bruce knew this, showing his men that he would not ask anything of them that he would not attempt himself.

The ladders were put in place, and Bruce was second over the town wall. While Bruce kept a band of men with him, ready to be sent where they were needed most, the rest spread out through the streets, dealing with any opposition. By sunrise Perth was won, and Bruce ordered the town walls toppled. (MAP A9)

There is no building left in Perth today from Bruce's time other than parts of St John's Church in the town centre. It is worth pointing out that some of the town walls survived till the 18th century. The castle stood at the end of the Skinnergate.

The moat that Bruce waded through has partially survived.

Perth still has the mill-lade that supplied water to turn the mill-wheels through many centuries, and this mill-lade also supplied the moats in Bruce's day. It can be seen where Mill Street meets Methven Street, but most of its route down to the Tay is through tunnels underneath later building work.

The Scots were able to continue their attacks on English garrisons and retake the castles and towns, not because England had changed its mind on the question of overlordship, but because it had problems of its own to deal with.

King Edward II had a favourite, Piers Gaveston, who was his 'boyfriend'. Edward foolishly made him an earl, thereby giving him status as a leader in times of war. The hereditary commanders were not very pleased that Gaveston could wield so much influence, not only over their lives but in affairs of state, and there was constant arguing. The roles were reversed for a change, with Scotland consolidating day by day.

Edward Bruce had taken Rutherglen, where the castle, which has totally disappeared, stood at what is now the junction of King Street and Castle Street. Dumfries Castle was taken. It stood where the modern Greyfriars Church is now.

There are still remains of Loch Doon Castle in Ayrshire which was also captured at this time, but they are not on the original site. When the loch level was to be raised as part of an extensive power scheme, the castle remains were moved block by block and rebuilt. They stand at the side of a small road which branches south-west down the loch's side from the A713, just south of Dalmellington.

The castle at Forfar stood on the Castlehill, a conical mound at the north-east end of the town. An old account states that it was 'stuffit all with Inglismen'. This castle was captured by Bruce and 'Philip, the forester of Plater'. Making an escalade under cover of night, they slew all the garrison, and 'brek doun the wall'.

The retaking of the castles was so successful that by the time of Bannockburn, only five were still in enemy hands. These were Berwick, Bothwell, Stirling, Jedburgh and Dunbar.

The siege of Stirling was in the charge of Edward Bruce. Stirling was unassailable on its high rock, and there seemed no way of capturing it by stratagem. Edward and his troops camped round about, having to content themselves with a waiting game – the castle food supplies could not last forever. This must have been somewhat galling for Edward. He was very much a fighting man, and would rather be out with a party of horsemen, hitting English patrols, than sitting down for a long siege.

Thomas Randolph, meanwhile, had proved himself such a brilliant soldier and of such value to Bruce that the title Earl of Moray was conferred upon him. The men of Moray (pronounced Murray) had been so stalwart in Scotland's cause that Bruce wished them to have a leader of their own.

James the High Steward of Scotland had died, and his son Walter was beginning to make a name for himself as a soldier. He came to Bruce's attention, and was another of the King's growing band of young and successful captains. Walter was also the heir to the lands of Renfrew, and commanded a large body of fighting men from the Glasgow and Paisley area.

Bruce had managed to oust nearly every Englishman from Scotland without having to fight a major battle. He had chipped away at the occupying forces without rattling cages too much in the south. His tactics had been to create a country that was so much bother for England that it would become too much of a drain on money, men and resources to be a viable gain.

But life has a way of twisting fate. 'The best laid plans of mice and men gang aft agley', as Burns said. News came that Edward Bruce had struck a deal with the governor of Stirling Castle. They had agreed that if a relieving force from England did not arrive within a year or so – the date specified was midsummer's day 1314 – the Castle would be handed over to the Scots. The governor would be aware that by then starvation would be the order of the day in his increasingly isolated situation, and the deal made sense to him. Edward Bruce was delighted – it meant that he was freed from camp life and overseeing the siege.

King Robert Bruce did not share his delight, however. He was furious as he realised the implications of this. England would see it as a direct challenge to its authority – nothing would be more likely to stop their internal bickering than this call to arms. It would be an opportunity to destroy Scotland once and for all. A major invasion was now imminent, and the foe far outnumbered anything Bruce could hope to put in the field.

But he soon swallowed his anger and started to think how English plans could be thwarted. All-out battle was out of the question. If the Scots lost, it would be the end of everything he had gained in the last seven years. And what of the captives held in English prisons?

Perhaps he could make life unbearable for the invaders. Employing the tactics he had perfected in the last few years – night attacks, severing supply lines and so on – might just work. He had a year to find out.

CHAPTER 9

Bannockburn

Events leading up to and including Sunday 23 June 1314

KING ROBERT BRUCE WAS RIGHT; his brother's deal at Stirling was seen as a direct challenge and the gauntlet was picked up at once. Edward II sent out summonses all over England and beyond. Letters requesting aid were sent not only to Wales and Ireland, but to France, Brittany, Poitou, Guienne and Germany, giving knights from foreign lands the chance to come and take their share of the spoil from Scotland once it had been trampled underfoot. One letter was even sent as far as Constantinople, asking for the release of the 'third best knight of Christendom' – Sir Giles d'Argentan, who had been imprisoned while going to fight at Rhodes on a crusade.

The meeting place and the date for the assembly of this vast army was named as Berwick on 10 June 1314. News of this would not be long in reaching Bruce's ears, and he sent out similar summonses, albeit on a much smaller scale, for a meeting in the Torwood during May 1314. Vestiges of the Torwood still exist, scattered around the village of the same name some five miles south-east of Bannockburn village.

Although Bruce had made his mustering date in May, it is probable that his captains were already busy teaching battle tactics to their own bodies of troops in readiness for conflict. Not that battle was a foregone conclusion – everything we know about Bruce shows that he was a man of caution, and would not have risked a single Scot's life unless absolutely necessary. Until full battle seemed tactically correct, he would have looked at every other avenue open to him. We know that Bannockburn was actually the least likely event of his whole war against England. It was never his plan to fight the military might of his southern neighbour. He had relied on guerrilla tactics and subterfuge to defeat their wealth of weaponry and numbers, and battle would be very much a last resort.

The numbers involved at Bannockburn on both sides have long been a bone of contention between historians. Accounts of numbers differ vastly. Some muster rolls exist to give a rough idea of manpower on the English side, but they are not conclusive. It is probably safe to guess that there were perhaps 20,000 footsoldiers and archers, and 2,500 heavy cavalry. Many thousands more would have made the trip north, however. Every army had its camp-followers, not to mention cooks, farriers, baggage train attendants, etc.

Bruce had perhaps 6,000 spearmen and 500 horse – but not heavy cavalry. His were much more lightly armed riders than their English counterparts, and were under the control of Keith, the Marischal of Scotland. This would put the English at a ratio of 3:1 against the Scots.

When Bruce's men assembled in the Torwood, drilling would have been the order of the day. He would have made sure his spearmen could move as a single entity on their captains' orders. Bruce had learned from Wallace at Falkirk, watching how his spearmen had kept charge after charge of armoured men and horses at bay. There were probably many present who had taken part at Falkirk sixteen years before. The vital difference was that Bruce's schiltroms were to be not only defensive, but offensive too. Wallace's had been static. Bruce's ranks of spearmen were taught to move in formation – like a giant hedgehog – across the field of battle. It would work, but only if the men were superbly trained and able to rely on their comrades without question.

From the time of mustering, Bruce's men had a month to wait until Edward II's appearance. Bruce would have had to organise the quarters and provisions for a month's stay well in advance, and every armourer in Scotland would have been busy creating the vast number of spears needed to equip the army. Imagine the scenes taking place all over the country. There would have been very few other topics of conversation. Everyone would have known of the English call to arms; everyone knew of the terrible threat this was to Scotland's very existence. On the plus side, Bruce's men had seen much action over the last few years. His captains had proved themselves in various campaigns, and morale must have been excellent.

The English massed at Berwick, with archers from Wales, footmen from Ireland, and soldiers of fortune with their heavy warhorses who had come from all over Europe. It must have been an awesome sight, the banners of the cream of chivalry fluttering above the shining armour. They marched north, following the old Roman road through Lauderdale, up over the high moor of Soutra in the Lammermuirs, and reached Edinburgh on 21 June.

Plaque at Bannockburn

Bruce, meanwhile, had moved his troops back towards Stirling, and positioned them on the ground where the Bannockburn Heritage Centre stands today. This belongs to the National Trust for Scotland. The 'Borestone', a carved boulder with a socket cut into it, stood on this site until recent times, and tradition states that Bruce rammed the shaft of the Lion Rampant banner into the boulder, to flap valiantly in the breeze. Its exact location was where the stairs are now, at the head of the footpath leading from the Heritage Centre to the concrete rotunda and flagpole. (MAP C32)

What remained of the Borestone was put inside the Heritage Centre when the rotunda was constructed in 1964, to save it from disappearing completely. For many years visitors had chipped souvenirs from it. Bob McCutcheon, bookseller of Stirling, who can trace his family back to the 1600s in the Bannockburn area, recalls hearing of an ancestor on his mother's side, a blacksmith whose premises stood in the vicinity of the Borestone, and who would hire out a hammer and chisel to tourists to chip keepsakes from the boulder. (This has been common practice at many landmarks connected with Scotland's history. I recall seeing a ring in Abbotsford near Melrose, the home of Sir Walter Scott, which had a polished stone that had come from the Borestone. Abbotsford also contains a cast of Bruce's skull, and a copy of a pair of candlesticks which are said to have belonged to Bruce.)

The flagpole, from which the Saltire flies, was raised to mark the spot where the Scots army stood to await the approach of the English. It was erected in 1870 by the Loyal Dixon Lodge of Dumbarton and the Rock of Hope Lodge of Stirling. The lower section is metal and the upper wood. It is topped by an axe, symbolising Bruce's favourite weapon. Its base was originally entwined in cast-iron thistles, and it was ringed by a mass of iron spears thrusting outwards to symbolise the spears of the schiltroms, but both thistles and spears were unfortunately removed during the building of the concrete rotunda in 1964. The original design of the rotunda was intended to depict an Iron-age broch, with entrance and exit stairs leading to and from an information hall, but this was never built.

A cairn has been erected to the Patriots of Scotland, and at the far side of the rotunda is the famous statue of Bruce by Pilkington Jackson. This shows Bruce astride his horse, battle-axe in hand, looking in the direction from which the English advanced. The facial features are a reconstruction made from a cast of Bruce's skull.

It was the raised piece of ground in the vicinity of the Borestone that saw the first disposition of Bruce's troops. An old Roman road ran through the Torwood, passing where Torwood

Bruce Statue at Bannockburn

Castle stands today, and crossing the Bannock Burn a few hundred yards south of the Borestone site. It was rightly assumed that the English army would approach by this ancient route. Bruce split his spearmen into four divisions of 1,500 men each, with the King's own division standing closest to the Bannock. The next division, standing nearer to Stirling, was under the command of Edward Bruce. The third was commanded by Douglas, with Walter the Steward taking part command. The fourth division was led by Randolph, Earl of Moray.

Bruce had his 500 horsemen under Keith slightly to the west of the schiltroms. In this vicinity stands a wooded stretch of higher ground, where Bruce sent his camp followers and various 'small folk'. The hill has taken its name from this, and is called Gillies Hill (*gillie* being the Gaelic for helpers or young men). The term 'small folk' certainly referred to various non-combatants, but not exclusively. There would have been many good fighting men among them. These would have been latecomers, and those who had not been present at the drilling of the schiltroms. Bruce would have held these men back, as the schiltroms depended on tight discipline.

Bruce had chosen his ground well. As it had never been his intention to bring his men to battle, and he was unsure of what to expect from the English advance, he had left an escape route where the Scots could seek safety if the worst came to the worst. There is still a road running across the front of Gillies Hill which continues up alongside the Bannock Burn, over a shoulder of Earl's Hill (with its transmitter), then drops down to the Carron Valley, emerging beside Sir John de Graham's castle. Sir John was a close comrade of Wallace, and had died on the field at Falkirk. From there, beside the modern Carron Valley Reservoir, an army could have swung west towards the mountain-girt Lennox, or east to Denny, to emerge at the rear of the English army.

There are naturally changes since Bruce's time, and these should be considered when walking the battlefield today. On the route to the Carron Valley, the Bannock Burn runs through North Third Reservoir which takes three million gallons of water daily from the Bannock. With later mill-lades and modern drainage, the Bannock is a much less formidable barrier than it was in 1314.

The English army, as expected, advanced along the Roman road through the Torwood and past where Muirmailing and West Plean farms now stand. We know that a squadron of heavily-armed horsemen had cut away from the main body of the English army and headed down onto the carseland (or flatland) beside the River Forth. It has always been assumed that this squadron, commanded by Sir Robert Clifford and Sir Henry Beaumont, had gone to relieve Stirling Castle, but the English were aware of the Scots' presence in the Borestone area, and it is possible that they were circling round behind the Scots' position. The squadron must have branched off fairly early, as once the English army reached the area of West Plean farm, they would have been visible from the Scots' position, and a troop swinging off would have been noticed. Down in the carse they were beneath the Scots' field of vision. It is Bob McCutcheon's considered opinion that another squadron branched off the main English host onto the higher ground to try and circle round, cutting off the Scots' line of retreat, and perhaps eventually link up with Clifford and Beaumont's men, circling round the Scots' positions in a pincer movement.

We know that the very first blow at Bannockburn was struck by King Robert Bruce himself. As Bruce was inspecting some of the defences in front of the Scots' positions, the first English knights suddenly burst out of the trees. One of these knights, Sir Henry de Bohun, spotted the circlet of gold that sat on top of Bruce's leather helmet, glinting in the sun. It was his chance for glory. He rode an armoured warhorse and was clad in the finest of personal armour. Bruce was on a garron, a little unarmoured pony, and had no weapon to hand but his battle-axe. De Bohun lowered his lance and charged straight at Bruce.

Bruce calmly sat his pony. His division on the hill above could see it all and held their breath, awaiting the impact. At the last moment Bruce side-stepped his mount, and as de Bohun's impetus took him on, Bruce stood in his stirrups and smashed his axe down. It cleaved through armour and bone. De Bohun's horse carried on for a few steps before clattering to the ground in gory ruin.

With a shout, others of Bruce's division ran forward, spears outstretched, and attacked the knights of the English vanguard with such rage that they soon turned tail and galloped from the field. The Scots moved forward in pursuit, but a blast from a horn recalled the well-trained spearmen and they returned to their ranks within the King's division. As Bruce made his way back uphill he was surrounded by some of his captains, who berated him for risking all. Bruce merely lamented his broken battle-axe which had shattered with the impact. He was no fool though, and knew that the moral of this David and Goliath situation which his men had just witnessed would not be lost on them. He led by example, and had given them the best one possible. The story would be passed from man to man back through his army, and would lose nothing in the telling.

Most writers are of the opinion that this confrontation took place in the area around the Roman road, just after it crossed the Bannock Burn, and de Bohun and his companions were out ahead of the main body of the English army. In Bob McCutcheon's reckoning, de Bohun's squadron was the other encircling arm, and this action took place a few hundred metres away from the usually assumed location. Local legend (and legends usually originate from some grain of truth) claims that the English came upon Bruce's men checking their defences on the opposite side of the burn, and that the clash between Bruce and de Bohun took place where the farm named Foot o' Green now stands. Foot o' Green supposedly got its name from Bruce standing in his stirrups, his horse rearing on its hind legs, and as it was such a small pony, Bruce's legs went down into the soft ground.

It must be remembered that there were many amongst the English host who would have been as familiar with the Stirling area as Bruce. Many of them would have campaigned in Scotland before, and all travellers to the north in those days would have ridden or marched along the old Roman road, heading for the bridge (if one was in existence after the Battle of Stirling Bridge), or the ferries and fords on the River Forth.

Meanwhile, Clifford and Beaufort's squadron of heavily armed horsemen were spotted down on the carse passing the last of the Scots' positions. Randolph's schiltrom was situated nearest St Ninians Church, and Bruce turned, expecting to see this schiltrom block the squadron's way. But he found Randolph standing at his shoulder. He rebuked Randolph for neglect of his duty, and Randolph, chastened, hurried back to his men and immediately marched them out in full view of the English horsemen.

The bold knights could not resist the challenge to ride right over the top of the advancing Scots, and quickly reined round their mounts, lowering their lances, and spurred them forward at a gallop. Randolph's men, spears bristling, formed their square and braced themselves for the impact.

During warfare in this era, it was believed that footsoldiers were no match for heavily-armed horsemen. Man and mount, both clad in armour, was the medieval equivalent of a tank, and charging several hundred strong, they would sweep all before them. It would take supreme discipline for a wall of footsoldiers to face this kind of attack without faltering. One man losing faith would open a gap through which a mailed knight could enter and wreak havoc.

Randolph's men held firm as the English horses smashed into them, impaling themselves on the Scots' spear-points. I can imagine the spearmen letting out a yell just before the impact of the English knights, partly in defiance, and partly to stiffen their resolve. The rest of the Scots army on the hillside above saw their comrades appearing to have been completely engulfed by the tide of English horses, but the wave of horses broke and ebbed, and they could see the square of spearmen intact, the knights eddying round. They attacked again and again, looking for weak spots, but could find none.

In frustration, the knights threw their weapons at the spearmen. Douglas, meanwhile, was so worried for Randolph that he begged the King to be allowed to take his men and help. Bruce hesitated, but then gave Douglas the go-ahead. As Douglas led his spearmen down the hill, he saw that the English attack seemed to be losing momentum. He immediately called his men to halt. He did not want Randolph's men to have to share their glory. Randolph had sensed the English uncertainty and barked the order for the spearmen to go on the offensive. With a yell and in strict formation, the Scots moved forward, smashing their way through the horsemen. The English assault disintegrated, and the knights galloped from the field.

Randolph's men, exhausted from their efforts, removed their helmets to cool themselves. They had lost only one man, whereas there were piles of dead and dying men and horses on the English side.

The Scots were ecstatic. The fact that a section of Bruce's spearmen could beat an equivalent body of heavy horse had proved that tactically Bruce's ideas were sound. This, coupled with Bruce's slaying of the better-equipped de Bohun, let the Scots see that an unexpected victory was within their grasp. When the reports got back to the English commanders, that peasant spearmen had annihilated a squadron of gentleman knights, they must have been incredulous. There had only ever been a couple of occasions in the past when foot-soldiers had repulsed heavy cavalry.

The scene of the fight between Randolph's schiltrom and Clifford and Beaufort's knights took place in the area of Stirling known today as Randolphfield. The offices of Central Region Police Headquarters stand on the left of the road called Newhouse that leads from St Ninians towards Stirling town centre. On

Stone at Randolphfield (1)

Stone at Randolphfield (2)

the area of grassland immediately in front of the police offices are two standing stones about 15 yards apart, one a little larger than the other. Traditionally they mark where Randolph's men held the English charge.

I had heard about these stones but was unsure of their situation. I called at the Police Headquarters and asked the policeman on duty if the standing stones in front of the building were the stones that marked the Randolph fight at Bannockburn. 'Ach, don't be stupid, son. That's just a couple of auld stones' was his reply. So, it seems the story is still more or less unknown even to local inhabitants. I recall discussing the stones with the Scots historian and author, Nigel Tranter, wondering if they had been put up to mark the location of the fight. Tranter assumed that even if the stones pre-dated the fight, Randolph may have used them as landmarks, telling his men to 'line up at the stones'.

Near Randolphfield there is a small plaque on the wall at the roadside which replaced an earlier cairn commemorating the murder of the Regent Lennox in 1571. A little closer to the town centre, on the opposite side of the road, is Viewforth, the offices of Stirling Council. Flanking the doorway of one of the buildings are half-lifesize statues of Wallace and Bruce.

The English host had halted somewhere on the old Roman road, south of the Bannock Burn. They knew that the main army of the Scots was ahead in the Borestone area. Legend states that Edward and some of his commanders rode to the top of an area of raised ground to view the Scots. This rocky viewpoint stands on the right as you drive from the roundabout at Junction 9 on the M9 down through Pirnhall towards the Bannock Burn. The tree-covered tor is named Craigford, and a house and a few cottages stand in front of it.

From this position Edward II could look over to where the flagpole stands today, and assess the strength of the Scots' position. He could see that their front was protected by Milton Bog. This bog was drained in 1841, but there is still a large reedy patch below the rotunda site. When the draining was carried out, spikes were discovered. They were calthrops, which are spikes that were scattered in front of horses with a view to maiming them. They were assumed to have been used by the Scots to thwart English charges at Bannockburn, but according to Bob McCutcheon, they were most likely made during the 1820 uprising (a workers' insurection which took place in the west of Scotland) by some of the many 'nailers' who were employed in the Bannockburn area at that time. When weapon searches were ordered, he thinks the nailers sank the calthrops in the bog to hide them. They were then discovered when the bog was drained and wrongly assumed to have been used at the Battle of Bannockburn. Certainly Barbour makes no mention of spikes. Iron was a scarce commodity in Scotland in the 14th century, and it is debatable whether it would have been used for anything but weaponry when arms were needed for battle.

Edward and his commanders decided that as it was late in the day, they would find somewhere to bivouac with a view to defeating the Scots the following day. The whole army swung eastwards, and headed down towards the carse of the Forth, keeping to the right of the Bannock Burn which flows from the Roman road down through a gorge with steep banks. They marched through the area known as Quakerfield and Newmarket where the A9 runs through Bannockburn Village, then down through the area of Station Road, and crossed the Bannock at the end of the gorge, in the region of the roundabout on the A91 distribution road.

To get the feel of the lie of the land, you can park at Milton, where the Glasgow Road crosses the Bannock Burn, and walk down the riverbank to Ladywell Park in the lower reaches of the gorge, then back up the path on the opposite side, cutting through streets where necessary. (A Stirling street map is a handy tool.) The barrier that this gorge would have created for an armoured host is immediately apparent.

The English made their camp in the area now covered by Pike Road and Balquidderoch Wood, behind Bannockburn High School and St Mary's Primary School.

Before modern drainage, this area was intersected by sluggish peaty streams, draining to the Bannock and Pelstream, useful for watering horses perhaps, but the English would have had to loot wood and doors from the surrounding habitations to make bridges to enable their horses to cross. Even small ditches would be impassable for armoured horses and their riders.

The English army spent a restless night on the edge of the carse, thinking that the Scots would mount a night attack. Bruce's tactics to date would have made this seem very probable. There were mutterings amongst the ranks, too, many unhappy with the previous day's losses against Bruce's men and the serious loss incurred against Randolph. But there was still no real doubt that they would win if battle were joined. They may have assumed that Bruce might move his army to another location under cover of darkness.

We know that Bruce was in a quandary. If he fought the English and was defeated, he would lose everything. If he retreated, he could at least continue to wage a guerilla campaign. But Scots who had been with the English defected during the short midsummer night, and they told Bruce that, if he really wished to achieve freedom for Scotland, the English seemed demoralised and he should mount an attack on the morrow. Bruce asked his captains for their advice. To a man they wanted battle.

Bruce must have looked out over the hundreds of cooking fires glowing in the English camp before issuing the order for attack at first light. He did not seek this fight, but now that it was before him, he would use all his abilities to fulfil his role as King of Scots and as their general.

Monday 24 June 1314

Just after 3am there would have been a lightening of the sky, the Ochil Hills across the Forth outlined in the dawn. I can sense the Scots standing silent, gripping their spearhafts, mouths dry, eyes fixed ahead, as Robert Bruce, their king, rode across their front, catching their eyes, giving a nod as he recognised men he had shared adventures with over the last few years.

Something of what he said then has come down to us, how he

asked his men to fight with all their hearts, to meet the enemy boldly with their spears. He told them of their advantages, how they had right on their side, how the English had come north to do nothing but increase their power; that they fought for their wives and children, for freedom, and for Scotland's very future. He said that if any man feared the fight ahead, he could go now, with no loss of face. Not one man moved.

The advance was sounded, and Edward Bruce, Douglas and Randolph marched their men forward, down the slope towards the English camp fires. There is a slight dip where Clark Street stands today, and as the schiltroms rose out of this, their line would have been in sight from the English camp below. Trumpets sounded, braying across the divide between the two armies in the still early morning air, then there would have been a hive of activity in the English camp, as men mounted their horses, and divisions were formed.

Bruce had kept his division in reserve on the hilltop. He would be looking down at the mustering in the English camp, watching the distance between it and his schiltroms grow smaller.

Edward of England saw them come on, unable to believe that the Scots really intended to fight the might of England on an open battlefield. Ingram de Umphraville, a Scot fighting with the English, stood at Edward's shoulder. He recommended that the English army should retire behind their tents; the Scots, eager for spoils, would break ranks to go in search of booty, whereupon the English troops could reform, charge and destroy them. Edward replied that he needed no ruses to defeat such scum.

The Breacbannoch

The Scots halted. The clerics displayed the Breacbannoch, a strangely carved silver case shaped like a little house. It was one of the country's holiest relics, and was said to contain bones of either St Andrew or St Columba. It can now be seen in the Museum of Scotland in Edinburgh. At sight of this, the whole army dropped on one knee to offer a solemn prayer to God for victory. Edward was ecstatic. He turned to his officers and said, 'See, the Scots have come to beg for mercy!' De Umphraville replied that they were indeed begging for mercy, not from Edward, but from their maker, and that these men were ready to win or die.

The English advance sounded, and they came forward up the escarpment, the heavy cavalry leading, thousands of footmen behind, mustering as much speed as possible to meet the oncoming line of Scottish spears. The impact probably happened somewhere in the region of the main Bannockburn to St Ninian's road, where Bannockburn High School stands today.

The horsemen threw themselves upon the leading ranks of spearmen, but the Scots held firm, and managed to push forward to fill any intervening gaps. Too late, the English heavy cavalry found they had no room to manoeuvre. The many thousands of English foot soldiers were still pushing ahead, unable to see what was happening, and constricted the cavalry even more. Knights on armoured horses are only effective if moving at full tilt. Here, in their thousands, they were hemmed in. The Scots, wielding their 12ft spears, were able to stab at them, and even if unable to pierce armour, could push them from their saddles, to fall in clanking ruin. A man, clad in a hundredweight of armour, falling several feet from his horse, would have been stunned at the very least. His chances of getting back on his feet in the press would be nil. The Scots would be ready to stab at eye slits or at any other armour-joints they could find. Many spearmen stabbed at the horses, and they would rear, throwing their riders. Frightened, wounded horses, seeking to be as far away as possible from those thrusting spear-points, would kick and buck their way through the troops behind them, causing mayhem. In his narrative, Barbour talks of pools of blood all over the field, the grass turning red and slippery with the gore.

Probably only one in twenty of the English army had come face to face with a Scot at this point, but numbers are of no avail if they cannot be used. The English had the gorge of the Bannock

Bannockburn 1314

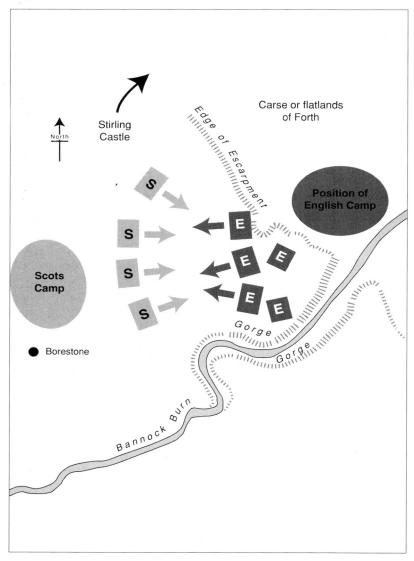

Stirling Castle

North

Edge of Escarpment

Carse or flatlands of Forth

Position of English Camp

S

S E

Scots Camp

S E E

S E E

● Borestone

Gorge

Gorge

Bannock Burn

on their left, and the pools of the carse to their rear. The ranks in the rear were still pushing forward to add to the confusion. The English command knew what had to be done. Orders were issued for the archers to gather on the right flank. The Scots' front was many men deep, and if the archers could mass, they needed only to keep firing into the Scots' ranks to open gaps that the English knights could take advantage of.

If you stand at Bannockburn High School and look over towards St Ninian's, there is a stretch of raised ground past Broom Road that is still free of buildings. Arrowheads have been found here, so it may be the spot where the English archers gathered. It would have made sense to commandeer a raised piece of ground, where the archers could see to clear their own troops.

Bruce watched from the top of the hill as they started to unleash their deadly hail. He knew how Wallace had used his spearmen to hold the English cavalry at Falkirk but had no reply to the murderous fire from the longbows. Wallace had no horsemen, as these had fled at the onset of the English attack. Bruce had learned a lesson from this, and he had kept back the 500 lightly armed horsemen under Keith in case of such a turn in events. These were unleashed down the hillside towards the archers.

With gathering momentum and room to cause the maximum amount of damage, these horsemen crashed through the ranks of archers, flailing left and right with swords, axes and maces. The English archers were going down like cut corn, and they turned and ran to find shelter in the mass of their countrymen still facing the Scots. Keith's horsemen were then free to harass the flanks and to run down any Englishmen who may have thought of leaving the field.

The Scots spearmen were silent with their exertions – they had no breath to spare to shout their war cries. They pushed against the mass of English, but they were heavily outnumbered, many of their opponents still fresh. The air was filled with the screams of injured men and horses.

Bruce brought his own schiltrom down the hill to add its

weight. Now the threat of the archers had gone, he no longer needed to keep his men in reserve. In his division were many high-landers who must have been champing at the bit to join the fight. He may have brought many of his men round to the enemy's right flank to push them towards the gorge of the Bannock Burn. They pushed their own spearmen from behind, making them move forward with renewed vigour – perhaps like a tug-of-war team, leaning forward, pushing with half steps, their outstretched forest of spears impenetrable. Bruce's reinforcements started a chant, which the rest took up with what breath they had: 'On them, on them, on them, they fail!'

The rear English ranks were starting to topple over the edge of the Bannock gorge. Some would be trying to climb down, but injured horses coming over the edge would crash into them. Others would be falling and taking down with them many of their fellows into the mud churned up by hundreds of feet. Barbour tells how the ground was saturated with the blood of the slain, the Bannock beginning to flow red.

The camp-followers had left their base at Gillies Hill, and come to the edge of the escarpment to watch the battle below. They could see the enemy beginning to buckle and men leaving the rear ranks to try and get away over the carse or over the gorge. The able-bodied men amongst these small-folk now showed some initiative. Making banners from blankets, they suddenly charged down the hill towards the conflict, shouting, 'Upon them now. They all shall die!'

The English were already wavering, and this shout from what seemed like a fresh division of troops was the last straw. Many tried desperately to extricate themselves from the crush, each man for himself. Bruce started chanting his battle cry and those about the King took it up. The enemy gave way more and more.

Edward of England, seeing his men starting to stream away, realised that the battle was lost. It was time to leave. With a tight-knit group around him, he broke free and started to gallop across the carse in the direction of Stirling Castle, hoping for safety. One of those with the King was Sir Giles d'Argentan, he who had come all the way from prison in Constantinople to take part in the battle. He informed Edward that he was not accustomed to running from a fight, and, reining his horse round, he charged back towards the Scots, only to go down under a hail of spear thrusts.

Their king gone, the English army disintegrated, and with the jubilant Scots pursuing, many were crushed underfoot, or drowned trying to cross the Forth. So many were slaughtered trying to cross the barrier of the Bannock gorge, and so high was the pile of the dead, that men could cross from one side to the other dryshod.

Edward of England, with his bodyguard of many knights, made his way to Stirling Castle. The governor refused him entry, saying he would have to hand over the Castle to the Scots or he would be besieged with no hope of rescue.

On the Castle esplanade is a statue of Bruce. It is one of those Victorian 'monstrosities' that portray Scotland's heroes as long-bearded and fat. The statue is 11ft high and was erected in 1877. It shows Bruce clad in chain armour looking towards Bannockburn as he sheathes his sword, and is the work of a sculptor named Currie

Leaving the castle, Edward had to circumnavigate the Scots, heading west to avoid them, then south. Barbour makes an interesting comment when he states that Edward made his escape travelling by the 'Round Table'. By this he means the landmark referred to today as the King's Knot. This strangely-shaped isometrical construction stands in the field beneath Stirling Castle rock, adjacent to the roundabout on the A811 where Dumbarton Road meets Albert Place. You can park nearby and wander over it, but a better view is gained by looking down on it from the Castle rock. A sign attributes it to the date of the Stewart Kings, but there is no doubt that

Bruce Statue, Stirling Castle

this is what Barbour's narrative refers to as the Round Table. (There have always been people who have argued that King Arthur was based in Scotland, and not in Cornwall at legendary Tintagel. There is Arthur's Seat in Edinburgh, and Camelon at Falkirk which some have identified as Camelot.)

English Edward was spotted, and word was soon brought to Bruce that the King of England was trying to escape, galloping for the border. Many refugees from the battle, having seen their king leave in the direction of Stirling Castle, had followed him and were clambering around the Castle rock. Although beaten and demoralised, they still comprised a sizeable force, and Bruce could not risk leaving them. He commanded Douglas to chase Edward, but could only give him sixty horsemen to pursue him and his knights.

Many other Englishmen made their way back to the Roman road and gathered there, probably at the site of their foremost supply wagons, unsure of what to do next due to lack of leadership. Legend states that a sizeable body of victorious Scots came across them and slaughtered them all. This spot went down in legend as the Bloody Fauld (fold).

To find this site, at the large roundabout at Junction 9 on the M9/M80 you take the A872 to Denny, and 100 yards from the roundabout a small farm road branches off on the left. Follow this road past its tight bend and continue for a few hundred yards past a stretch of woodland on the left. As you cross the little burn at the woodland's edge, the Bloody Fauld is on your right. It may only be a field, but it is a famous location in the history of the area.

Many small parties of English soldiers escaped the battlefield, and tried to make their way home, heading for the border, but the people of Scotland had many scores to settle with the hated invaders, and the ordinary folk waylaid many of them. Hundreds of incidents involving courage and horror must have taken place in the miles between Stirling and the border with England.

Douglas caught up with the English King and his bodyguard,

but it was too big a group to take on in a straight fight. He hung on their tails all the way to Winchburgh where Edward paused and Douglas did likewise, following again as soon as the English moved on, any stragglers being taken by Douglas's men. They were so well shadowed, in fact, that in Barbour's expressive phrase:

He kept them within such close measure
Allowing them not so much leisure
As to make water.

There have always been those in Scotland who put another nation before their own, and this happened when Edward reached Dunbar Castle, and Earl Patrick, a Scot, opened the door and gave him asylum. Edward was able to take a boat from Dunbar to Bamburgh in Northumberland. His capture would have saved many years of bloodshed, and his ransom would have secured Scotland's freedom.

Dunbar Castle's scant remains stand at the harbour. It was built on several rock stacks connected by stone-covered walkways, built like bridges. The last of these only collapsed in the late 20th century. Dunbar Castle has a later claim to fame when it was brilliantly defended against the English by Black Agnes, the daughter of Randolph.

Some of the foremost of England's military commanders, including the Earl of Hereford and several Scots, made their way to Bothwell Castle on the Clyde after escaping from the battlefield. Once they were inside, the constable, another Scot who held an English command, promptly turned the key and handed them over to Bruce.

Hereford's ransom alone returned to Bruce his Queen, Elizabeth, his daughter, the Princess Marjorie, his sister, Mary, who had been kept in a cage by Edward Longshanks, and his good friend and confidant, Bishop Wishart of Glasgow. Wishart was old and blind, but he had survived to revel in the great victory of

Bannockburn after his years of faithful support for Wallace, then Bruce. He did not survive for long. His tomb lies defaced, unloved and forgotten, without even a sign, at the rear of the crypt in Glasgow Cathedral. (MAP C28)

Bothwell Castle stands above the Clyde, near the towns of Bothwell and Uddingston from both of which it is signposted. It is in the care of Historic Scotland, and a small fee is charged for entry, but even a walk round its perimeter cannot fail to make one marvel at the quality of workmanship of the medieval masons. Its central keep, the Great Donjon, though partly ruined, gives even more of an insight into their skill when you see the thickness and construction of the walls. Since the castle became derelict, people have carved their names within its precincts, among them a youthful David Livingstone, the explorer, who was born in Blantyre just a little upstream on the other side of the river. (MAP C29)

Many of the poor in Scotland suddenly came into great wealth with the spoils of the battle. The knights who fought for England, expecting an easy victory, had brought north with them a fortune in silver and gold, plates, silks, money and other goods. Good horses also became plentiful. Many a peasant farmer must have returned home on some great lord's warhorse.

The spoil was taken to Cambuskenneth Abbey and the weaponry alone must have formed mighty piles. The armour taken from the dead would have equipped most of the knightly classes of Scotland. (MAP C33)

I wonder what the ordinary spearman felt like after the battle. The names and tales of the foot soldiers of Bruce's army are lost forever, but how I would like to hear an eye-witness account from one of them. I can imagine a highlander making his way on foot back to his glen, clasping a much better sword than the one he had left with, carrying silver plates bearing some earl's coat of arms as his prize, breaking into a run for the last mile or two, hardly able to wait to inform his family and friends of the victory. I can picture him entering his village, people looking up as he appeared, and him shouting, 'We beat them! We beat them good and proper!' in the Gaelic.

Bannockburn the Battle had been won, but the pride of Edward II and England would not let him concede Scotland's right to nationhood. The war had a long time to run and many Scots would lose their lives before his arrogance would let him admit defeat.

England gained one thing from the outcome of the battle, however. As Edward II was fleeing, he made a vow to the knights around him that if he escaped the clutches of Douglas and the rest of the Scots, he would found a college in gratitude, and thus England has us to thank for Oriel College, Oxford.

Invasions and Alarms

KING ROBERT BRUCE BEHAVED with such magnanimity towards many of the captives at Bannockburn that it even drew comments from English chroniclers. This was not only extended to captives. The bodies of two of England's foremost captains, Gloucester and Clifford, were returned to England for honourable burial.

The shock of Bruce's victory rippled over Europe. The story of how his spearmen had defeated the chivalry of England was to change the tactics of many future battles. His genius earned Bruce the epithet First Knight of Christendom.

As soon as it was discovered that England was still claiming overlordship of Scotland, and that the defeat of its army had altered nothing, it was decreed that regular invasion of the northern shires of England to bring back booty would be the order of the day, although it would make little impact on England as a whole. The devastation of Cumbria and Northumbria, which were vulnerable and undefended, over the next few years would depopulate those shires terribly, and ransoms taken for immunity from destruction would help to replenish Scotland's coffers.

Bruce's tactics of fighting on foot – a necessity in Scotland because of a lack of suitable horses – plus his ability to use the land itself as a ally, prompted the writing of a **verse**, 'Good King Robert's Testament'. Translated into understandable English, it runs as follows:

On foot should be all Scottish war
By hill and moss themselves to rear
Let wood for walls be bow and spear
That enemies do them no deir (harm)
In safe places go keep all store

And burn the plainland them before
Then shall they pass away in haste
When they shall find the land in waste
With wiles and wakings of the night
And great noises made on height
Then they shall turn, made great afraid
As though they were chased with sword away
This is the council and intent
Of Good King Robert's Testament.

Bruce had turned forty, and as his wife, Elizabeth, had spent what should have been her most productive child-bearing years in an English prison, and the chances of her mothering a future heir were unknown, the question of the succession to the throne of Scotland was discussed at a parliament held at Ayr in April 1315. This took place at St John's Church, the tower of which still stands in a grassed area among the houses between the shore and Fort Street, just off Seabank Road.

It was decided in the circumstances to confer the right to the crown on Edward, Bruce's brother, then on his heirs. Failing this, the crown was to go to Bruce's daughter Marjorie, then to her heirs. To ensure the succession, her hand was granted in marriage to Walter the Steward, or Stewart, who had distinguished himself at Bannockburn. This marriage between young Walter and Marjorie, who would have been around twenty, was to result in the Stewart dynasty that would one day rule Scotland and inherit the throne of England via James VI and I. It was agreed that Randolph, Earl of Moray, would act as Regent if any future heir was a minor.

On a different tack, Edward Bruce, now Earl of Carrick, was approached by the O'Neills of Ulster, and offered the crown of Ireland. The Irish were just as disenchanted with English rule as the Scots, and the success of Bannockburn was obviously the catalyst behind what might seem to us today an extraordinary move. It may not be so extreme when looked at from the point of view of the people of the early 14th century. The Bruces, as natives of Carrick, probably had strong ties and communications with the people of Ireland, lying just across the sea, and the fact that the Irish and Scots came from the same blood ancestry was probably more important then.

To threaten England's western approaches must have appealed to Bruce as a way to bring pressure to bear on Edward, and he backed this audacious plan.

Edward Bruce set sail for Ireland with a sizeable body of men and landed at Larne on 26 May 1315. Randolph, Earl of Moray, accompanied him, perhaps travelling on Bruce's orders as a calming influence on Edward's hot-headedness. Randolph was also a brilliant soldier.

Their first objective was the capture of Carrickfergus Castle. Carrickfergus, immediately across the channel from the homelands of the Bruce family, would provide a strong base and supply depot for Edward Bruce's forays into southern Ireland in his endeavour to consolidate his hold on the country.

Although there is no doubt that this invasion of Ireland would very much have disconcerted the English, it was never going to be a straightforward task to unite the Irish, who, if anything, were even more clannish than the Scots, with in-fighting the norm. They seemed to be more content fighting one another than uniting against the common foe. This was a problem with Celtic peoples in general, and Anglo-Saxons, being a different kettle of fish entirely, always saw the advantages of such a situation, making the old adage, 'divide and conquer', their maxim for ruling their neighbours.

Bruce's personal strength had obliterated this weakness in Scotland. He had ideas of trying to consolidate Ireland, and, if this were successful, perhaps moving on into Wales in the hope of creating a kind of Pan-Celtic organisation more capable of withstanding English claims of superiority and overlordship. But, alas, this was not to be.

Carrickfergus did eventually fall to the Scots, and Edward

Carrickfergus Castle

Bruce made several forays into the southern half of Ireland. On some of these King Robert Bruce accompanied him, bringing extra manpower and the advantage that his personal presence would give to the campaign.

Four real incursions were made into the south. On the first, from May to September 1315, Edward Bruce struck far enough south to sack Dundalk, Ardee and Louth, before being confronted by an army led by the Anglo-Irish Earl of Ulster. He retreated north, drawing the Earl after him, then completely routed the Earl's forces at the battle of Connor, some twenty miles north-west of Belfast.

Heading south again during November 1315, he managed to get as far as Castledermot (on the N9), before retiring slightly to face an impressive army commanded by Edmund Butler. They came face to face at the mote of Ardskull, near the town of Athy. Although outnumbered, Edward Bruce was the victor, but a bad famine was ravaging Ireland, and he again moved back to the sanctity of the north. Around this time he was crowned High King of Ireland.

His next foray was during the spring of 1317, when he had more success, and was accompanied by King Robert Bruce. Their march south caused a panic in Dublin, where the locals even

The Bruce Campaigns in Ireland

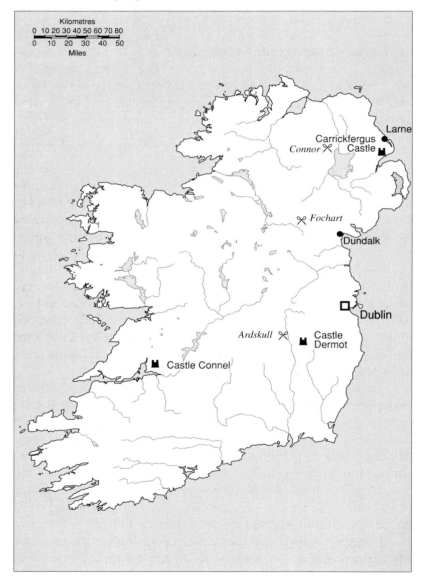

burned some of the houses outside the city walls to deny the Scots shelter during their expected attack. Although the Scots halted at Castleknock on the outskirts, they by-passed Dublin to strike as far west as Castleconnell on the River Shannon. Famine was rife, local support did not materialise, and a retreat northwards was again the order of the day. King Robert Bruce returned to Scotland, and little is known of Edward Bruce's movements till his final battle at Fochart, just north-west of Dundalk, on 14 October 1318.

The Lanercost Chronicle states that his army was split into three separate columns of march, so far apart that there was no communication between them. A much stronger force of the enemy was able to deal with the first and second columns as separate entities, and when the third, led by Edward Bruce himself, came up, it too was overwhelmed. He was killed fighting amongst his men. When his body was found, it was beheaded then quartered, to be displayed in various parts of Ireland. There is no record of the fate of any of Edward Bruce's remains.

King Robert Bruce must have done more than a little soul-searching when the news of the demise of his brother reached him. All four of his brothers were now dead, but at least in Edward's case he had died with sword in hand, and not at the hands of some English torturer. A parliament was held at Scone on 3 December 1318 to ratify the change of succession to the throne.

The Scots had learned to battle on foot to counter the heavy cavalry of their opponents, and they developed other tactics for their continued incursions into northern England. These raids became more and more daring, some probing as far south as Yorkshire, and speed was of the essence in order to appear deep in enemy territory before any warning could be given.

For these ploys the Scots carried only the bare essentials, and used sturdy little native ponies, called hobins, from which the riders earned the moniker 'hobelars'.

We know so very little about the day-to-day life of the people of Scotland during the Wars of Independence that it is good to come across little snippets of real information. Jean le Bel, a knight from Liäge who fought as an English mercenary against the Scots, wrote a chronicle in later life. He described how lightly-armed Scots horsemen carried iron plates, or griddles, behind their saddles. They also carried small sacks of oats. The griddles could be placed over a fire, and a handful of oats mixed with water to make a kind of cake – an oatcake – which was baked on the griddle. He also mentioned that the Scots would sometimes cut a vein on a rustled cow, and mix the blood with oats before cooking it – an early black pudding. (Oatcakes and black pudding are still enjoyed by the Scots, along with haggis which is a mixture of offal and oats cooked in a sheep's stomach.)

With regard to the future of Scotland on a dynastic basis, Princess Marjorie Bruce was pregnant, and was probably residing on her husband's family lands which lay around Renfrew. The castle at Renfrew, although long gone, stood to the west of the road that leads from the town centre to the Clyde. Parts of the fosse, or ditch, surrounding it were still visible in 1775.

Marjorie's pregnancy was well advanced when she was thrown from her horse near Knock Hill, which was somewhere between Paisley and Renfrew. It is not known whether she was killed and her child (who became Robert II) was born by caesarian section, or whether she went into early labour and died in childbirth. Marjorie was only in her early twenties, and had spent much of her life in an English prison. (MAP C30)

The spot where she was thrown was later marked by a pillar which stood on top of some stone steps. The pillar was octagonal, with an eight-sided base. Sometime between 1779 and 1782 the monument was destroyed by a local farmer, who, in his ignorance, used the pillar as a door lintel and the stones of the supporting steps to repair gaps in a wall. The area is now built over, but the site is marked by a cairn, with a plaque which tells the story. This cairn was raised by the father of Iain Hamilton, one of those responsible for 'liberating' the Stone of Destiny from Westminster Abbey in 1950. I have shown the cairn to many people who live

Arbroath Abbey
Scene of the signing of the famous 'Declaration of Arbroath' in 1320.

Melrose Abbey

A favourite of Bruce's, his heart is buried within the Abbey Grounds.

Carlisle

Many Scots including Bruce's brothers met a gory end here.

Musselburgh
An old view of the 'Honest Toon' where Randolph died.

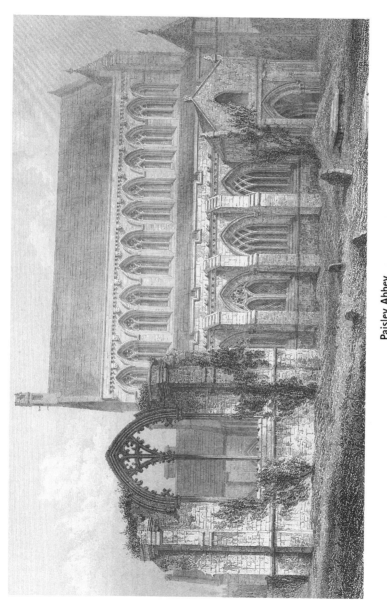

Paisley Abbey
Bruce's daughter Marjorie is buried within.

Lochmaben

A famous border stronghold at the time of the Wars of Independence.

The Pass of Brander
Bruce defeated the MacDougalls here in a hard fought battle.

Seal, coins and skull of King Robert Bruce
Old print showing artefacts of Bruce.

nearby and they have all been surprised to discover it, so it would seem to be little known. It stands on the right of the Renfrew Road, travelling from Paisley to Renfrew, on the edge of the housing scheme called Gallowhill, a few hundred yards south of where Renfrew Road crosses the M8 motorway.

Marjorie was buried in Paisley Abbey, where a tomb said to be hers, stands inside the church. This tomb had been demolished and the parts moved outside on the orders of the Duchess of Beaufort who wanted the chapel where the tomb stood for Church of England services. Luckily, the parts of the tomb were collected and it was rebuilt by the good Dr Boog, a minister of Paisley, around 1830.

Cairn to Marjorie Bruce, Paisley

Paisley Abbey is open to the public. It is a stunning building, well worth visiting. It is the last resting place of all the High Stewards of Scotland. Robert III, Marjorie's grandson, is also buried there. There are plaques giving the details of historic events, and excellent stained glass including the Wallace Window. William Wallace was probably schooled at the Abbey.

While Edward Bruce had been active in Ireland, James Douglas was carving out a huge slice of history for himself with various daring acts. The only stronghold the English still held in Scotland was Berwick. It was at this time the largest town in Scotland, and not only could it be easily provisioned from the sea, its proximity to England meant that its relief from a siege would not be difficult. More importantly, after the Sack of Berwick carried out by Longshanks in 1296, a large proportion of the townsfolk would have been English incomers, who would have bolstered the garrison in times of trouble.

With a big town to feed, a large foraging party left Berwick to raid through Teviotdale and the Merse, which is the arable flatland between Berwick and Kelso. The party was strengthened by the presence of Gascon knights in the pay of England. Douglas, with a body of men, was in Selkirk Forest when word came to him of these activities. He and his men galloped in pursuit, coming across the enemy at Scaithmuir, north of Coldstream, on 14 February 1316. It is reported that Douglas's party was outnumbered two to one, but did not hesitate to attack. A bloody, drawn-out battle followed, with the Scots only getting the upper hand after Douglas slew Cailhau, the Gascon leader. Douglas is reported to have said after the fight was won that it was the hardest battle he had ever taken part in. The battle site is two miles due north of Coldstream, on a farm by the name of Skaithmuir (pronounced by the locals 'Scay-muir').

Douglas had built himself a headquarters near the border, at Lintalee, close to Jedburgh. It stood on the spit of land between the meeting of the Jed Water and Lintalee Burn. He heard of the approach of a large body of English soldiers, and although heavily outnumbered, attacked them as they entered woodland after crossing the border at Carter Bar. At the point where the road drops to enter the forest south of Lintalee, Douglas got his men to fire a volley of arrows into the front ranks of the English troops. The Scots then came out of the trees and struck quickly at the leading ranks, Douglas himself slaying the commander, before disappearing back into cover. The enemy were so disheartened that they retreated in disorder.

Douglas and his men returned to his headquarters at Lintalee to find that another English patrol had taken over in their absence. These too were dealt with in no uncertain terms, with the result that Englishmen began to speak of the 'Black Douglas' as some kind of bogeyman. North Country Englishwomen would sing their children to sleep with:

Hush ye, hush ye, little pet ye,
Hush ye, hush ye, do not fret ye,
The Black Douglas shall not get ye.

It was said that much of the fear that leapt into Englishmen's hearts at even the mention of Douglas's name stemmed from his practice of not slaying his prisoners out of hand. He would give them the choice of losing a hand or an eye, to ruin their usefulness in battle. This only served to make his legend grow all the more.

Just after the affair at Lintalee, Robert Neville of Raby, whose nickname was the 'Peacock of the North', decided he had heard enough of this Douglas, and joining the garrison at Berwick, announced that he would be happy to fight Douglas under any circumstances. Douglas was happy to take on the challenge, and planted his standard outside the walls of Berwick.

The Peacock rode out with a body of followers, including three of his brothers, and took up a hilltop position. Douglas and his followers immediately charged to the attack, and a hard fight ensued with Douglas slaying the Peacock, and his three brothers being taken for ransom. After this, very few Englishmen entertained the idea of meeting Douglas in combat.

Soon after this, Berwick fell to the Scots. Keith, the Marischal of Scotland, had a relative called Sim of Spalding, who was one of the garrison of Berwick, and he contacted Keith to inform him that he would enable the Scots to enter the town at an agreed time. Keith took the news to Bruce, and he sent Randolph and Douglas to Berwick. On the night of Saturday, 1 April 1318, Sim of Spalding was in command of the section of the wall at the Cowgate, where he turned a blind eye to the Scots' scaling ladders being hooked on to the walls. The Scots took the town after heavy street fighting, but the castle held out for another eleven weeks before its garrison was starved into surrender. At last, Scotland was Bruce's in its entirety.

Around the time that Berwick was taken, St Andrews Cathedral was completed after 150 years of building work. Bruce attended the opening ceremony, which must have been a proud day for Bishop Lamberton. Sadly, this building was utterly destroyed at the Reformation, but a visit to the ruins gives some impression of the magnificence of its scale. (MAP A10)

When Bruce was sending raiding parties into northern England to extract protection money and take goods from various

St Rule's Tower, St Andrews

towns, the English were also making forays north to test the mettle of his soldiers. A fleet of ships made a landing in the Inverkeithing area of Fife, and the soldiers tried to cow the local inhabitants, feeling safe in the knowledge that the Scots' forces were concentrated elsewhere.

The local Scots soldiers, under the Sheriff of Fife, took fright at the size of the invasion force, and started to retreat before them. They got as far as Auchtertool before they met with Bishop Sinclair of Dunkeld, who, on finding out the circumstances, berated the Scots, accusing them of cowardice. He seized a lance and rode off in the direction of the English. His example caused a change of heart amongst the Scots soldiers and they turned and went after him, and killed many of the invaders. The English hurried back to their boats. Many were wearing heavy armour and some were drowned after one of the overladen boats capsized, throwing them into the Forth.

The taking of Berwick spurred the English on, and Edward II, joining forces with the Earl of Lancaster, marched a large army of some 8,000 to the border to re-take the town. Bruce, expecting an English show of strength, had given the captaincy of Berwick to his son-in-law, Walter Stewart. His trust was well founded. Walter managed to repulse the attacks by the English, but he could not hold out indefinitely against such a large force.

Bruce sent Douglas and Randolph to Berwick's relief. They looked at the English dispositions, and realised that this was too much for them to deal with in open confrontation. They knew that most of the English troops were from the northern shires, however, and hit upon a plan. They took their hobelars south, and began to ravage the countryside, striking down into Yorkshire. The rumour was spread that they intended to capture the English Queen, whom Edward II had left in York while he attacked Berwick.

Word was brought to the Archbishop of York that the Scots

were as near as the village of Myton on the River Swale, some ten miles north-west of York itself. The Queen of England was hurriedly removed further south to the safety of Nottingham, while Archbishop Melton raised a force to deal with the Scots. Many of the able-bodied fighting men were already absent at the siege of Berwick, but the Archbishop assembled a collection of prelates, townsfolk, and farmers, to march out and deal with Douglas and Randolph. It must have escaped the Archbishop's notice that he was dealing with the two of the greatest soldiers in Europe who could not be surprised or put to flight easily. After all, much of Bruce's regular fighting force were veterans of many years of war; most would have been present at Bannockburn, and they would have been inured against taking fright at the thought of the forthcoming conflict.

The English crossed the bridge over the Swale at Myton to find a cloud of thick smoke wafting across their front; the Scots had ignited some piles of damp hay. They came through the smoke to find the Scots drawn up in schiltrom formation. The Scots let out a huge yell of defiance, and panic took over in the Archbishop's army. They ran back through the smoke, the spearmen at their heels, only to find a group of Scots hobelars had taken control of the bridge, and escape was impossible.

It was a massacre, not a battle. It was said the Swale claimed far more English lives than the steel of the Scots, many having jumped into the river in their haste to escape. Because of the number of casualties among the clergy, the Scots called this incident derisively 'The Chapter of Myton'. (MAP B1)

A great deal of booty was taken by the Scots. As Archbishop Melton had carried so much treasure and church plate with him, pleas were later made to no fewer than thirty-one religious houses to raise funds to replace the loss.

When word of what had happened reached the besiegers in Berwick, coupled with all the reports of the burning and harrying of the countryside, there was near mutiny in the English camp. The army at Berwick decamped and headed south immediately.

Randolph and Douglas headed north, slipping by the returning English, burning the surrounding countryside en route.

Myton-on-Swale is a prosperous but sleepy little place today and it is hard to equate it with the Chapter. The road which leads to it goes nowhere else, so it is very much a backwater. It is best reached from the A19 Thirsk to York road. There is still a bridge across the Swale, used for nothing more than farm access. The bridge may be several hundred years old, but as the Chapter took place in the adjacent field, if it is of later construction, it is on the site of the original.

The Swale is a deep, sluggish, ditch-like river, not particularly wide, but it would be a formidable barrier in any circumstances. As you cross the bridge, in the field to your left is where the Scots attacked Archbishop Melton's force. The name used locally for what happened is 'The White Battle', probably a reference to the number of clergy involved. If you stand at the bridge-end, looking out over the field, you get a feeling of how it must have been on the day. The countryside is very fertile and must have produced rich pickings for 14th-century marauders. It is extremely flat, too, and very much 'England'.

In York there are several shops which sell artefacts, many found locally by people using metal detectors, and I have no doubt the field where the Chapter took place has been scoured again and again. In one shop I picked up a coin from the reign of William the Lion, and the proprietor said it had been found locally with a metal detector. How did it come to be lost so far south? We shall never know, just as we shall never know the names of the ordinary men-at-arms who were present at the Chapter of Myton. I would love to have heard them telling the story over a beer in the tavern when they returned to Scotland. It is a shame that all those stories, all those heroes, all those acts of individual courage which would have been passed down through families for a generation or two, simply disappeared. I constantly meet people through shared historical interests who say, 'If only I could see back, just for a few seconds, to see how it really was.'

Bruce had to try to find a way of influencing the minds of the southern English in order to get them to recognise Scotland's right to freedom. He could hammer at the northern counties ad infinitum, but it would mean very little to the power base centred around London. Like many later politicians, people in the south thought even northern England was remote, let alone some outlandish country like Scotland.

Bruce would have to use the finest brains in his kingdom to endeavour to find other ways to exert pressure.

Declaration and Intent

DOCUMENTATION IS NOT REALLY what this book is about, but an exception has to be made for the Declaration of Arbroath. It is not only one of the outstanding documents of Scottish history, but of world history too. Even the American Declaration of Independence owes a big nod in its direction.

Bruce knew that the one thing that would have an effect on the untouched south of England was the influence of the Pope. The Vatican was the most influential powerbase of the known world, and monarchs generally paid heed to its orders – but not in Scotland. The Pope had excommunicated Bruce after his murder of the Red Comyn, and then excommunicated the country of Scotland for not accepting English rule, but the Scots turned a blind eye to that.

Bruce was fortunate in the churchmen of his time. People like Wishart and Lamberton were mainstays of the independence struggle, and another name to be added to the list is that of the Abbot of Arbroath, Bernard de Linton. It is believed he was responsible for the final draft of the Declaration.

The document is the epitome of all that is admirable in patriotism. It speaks of a man's right to freedom and his right to defend it. It speaks of Scotland, that wee country on the edge of the world, and of its people who desired nothing but the chance to live in peace. It is a lengthy document, but some of it must be quoted here.

> We have been freed from so many and so great evils by the valour of our Lord and Sovereign, Robert Bruce. Like Judas Maccabeus or Joshua, he gladly endured every danger to save his people and kingdom from their enemies . . . our common and just consent have made him our King, because through him our salvation has been wrought . . .

If he should give up our cause and yield us to England, we would cast him out as the enemy of us all, and choose another king who should defend us. For so long as only a hundred of us remain, we will never yield to the dominion of England.

WE FIGHT NOT FOR GLORY NOR WEALTH NOR HONOURS, BUT FOR FREEDOM ALONE WHICH NO GOOD MAN SURRENDERS BUT WITH LIFE ITSELF.

Bernard de Linton, seven centuries on and in a technological age, I salute you. There are basic rules to life that remain constant, and you have clarified them for me.

This document was revealed at a parliament held at the Abbey of Arbroath on 6 April 1320. Eight earls and thirty-one barons added their seals to it, so that it could be seen to contain the will of the people, rather than the dictate of their sovereign. It was to be used to bring papal pressure to bear on England to recognise Scottish independence, and to try and ensure a lasting peace. It did not immediately bring any conclusion to Scotland's troubles, but it stands as a beacon to man's basic freedom, to shine through the intervening centuries as a strength for Scots men and women to draw on when their existence was threatened.

The Abbey at Arbroath, like so many ecclesiastical buildings, has suffered badly over the centuries, particularly at the hands of the reformers. It was founded by King William the Lion of Scotland in 1178, and was not completed till 1233. King William was interred under the high altar. The Abbey stands in the High Street, where even in its state of ruin, it overshadows the town, the ruins being 275ft long and 67ft broad. They are in the care of Historic Scotland and open daily to the public. (MAP A11)

The year 1320 was memorable for King Robert Bruce. His Queen, Elizabeth, mothered a child, a girl who was named Maud. They had probably despaired of ever becoming parents after the Queen's long imprisonment, but they could now hope for more children, the succession requiring as many as possible.

At the end of the following year, 1321, the English Earl of Lancaster was becoming exasperated at the repeated incursions into northern England, and, seeing no help forthcoming from the monarchy or from the powerful lords in the south, he entered into secret negotiations with Randolph, Douglas and Bruce, to try and rectify the situation. Lancaster raised an army, and was on his way to join the Scots when he was intercepted by Andrew Harcla, soon to be Earl of Carlisle. Harcla defeated Lancaster's army as they crossed the River Ure at Boroughbridge on 16 March 1322, and Lancaster was executed shortly afterwards. This was unfortunate, as an English rebellion could have proved beneficial for the recognition of the Scots' sovereignty. Boroughbridge was an English battle, fought on English soil, but it took place less than three miles west of the site of the Chapter of Myton. The site of the battle is north of the town of the same name, just east of the B6265.

A similar fate to Lancaster's later befell Harcla, as he also entered into negotiations with the Scots to try and find a solution to the constant bloodshed. He was accused of treason and executed.

After the Pope received the Declaration of Arbroath, he sent envoys to Edward II, to enquire about making a lasting peace with Scotland. Unfortunately, Edward of England saw Harcla's victory at Boroughbridge as a good omen and he mounted another huge invasion force to finally conquer Scotland. This army mustered at Newcastle on 24 July 1322, and began to march north. The main Scots army was withdrawn north of the Forth and was stationed at Culross in Fife. Bruce used the well-tried tactics of 'Good King Robert's Testament', and laid waste the countryside in advance of the huge host, clearing the Borders and the Lothians of livestock and people.

The English burned Melrose and Dryburgh Abbeys. They moved north, reached Edinburgh, and burned the Abbey of Holyrood. But disease was rife amongst the soldiers and starvation was setting in. All the English foraging parties had been able to find was one skinny lame cow in the cornfield of the village of Tranent east of Edinburgh. On seeing it, the Earl of Surrey remarked that it was the dearest beef he had ever seen, as it must have cost a thousand pounds to find. The proud army was reduced to a sorry rabble, and although Edward II had boasted that this was to be the end of Scotland, he had to give the order for retreat. As they retired south through the Melrose area, Douglas saw his chance, and attacked part of the army, his dreaded war cry of 'Douglas! Douglas!' striking fear in the enemy. The word spread that Douglas was at their heels and this would hasten many Englishmen back over the border.

At this point Bruce once again showed his military genius, matching that of his statesmanship.

Bruce had many men at his disposal at Culross and elsewhere, and he took this host, which included many highlanders, south by the Solway fords to strike south-eastwards by the often-used route of the Eden Valley to appear in Yorkshire, hard on the heels of the retreating English. The Scots arrived in Northallerton around 12 October 1322, and discovered that Edward of England was lodged in Rievaulx Abbey, twenty miles to the south-west. (MAP B3)

An audacious plan formed in Bruce's head to contrive to capture the King of England in person, Surprise was the Scots' best weapon, but the Hambleton Hills stood between the Scots army and Edward at Rievaulx. The main English force was positioned on top of these hills.

The Hambleton Hills are not hills in the Scottish sense. They are more a huge plateau rising sheer out of the Yorkshire plain, with a reasonably level summit many miles across. They are very imposing, with panoramic vistas from the top. Bruce approached them from the direction of Thirsk, and would have been assessing the strength of the English army. It was decided that a frontal assault should be made. Bruce chose Douglas to lead this attack, while he stayed back to direct operations. Randolph had no particular orders to follow, and must have asked Bruce if he could join Douglas's attack, because as Douglas started to inspect his troops, he spotted Randolph grinning back at him from the front row. Douglas immediately invited Randolph to help lead the assault.

Historians are mostly in agreement that the encounter took place on the escarpment between Whitestone Cliff in the north, and Roulston Scar, two miles to the south. In his work on Bruce, Professor Barrow places the fight there. Even Barbour, writing in the 1370s, speaks of the English blocking 'the path' up 'the brae', which must be the route of the modern A170, which climbs in zigzags to the edge of the summit plateau. (MAP B2)

Standing there, looking at the patchwork of fields far below, it is astonishing that it would be possible for men to fight their way up such a gradient, boulders bouncing down, arrows winging past. It is entertaining enough watching trucks and lorries trying to negotiate the steep hills and the twists and turns the modern road has to take. I have to say that I have my doubts about the validity of the frontal assault taking place at this spot, even though all the pointers indicate that this was indeed the case.

With Bruce watching from below, an assault was mounted, and hard fighting ensued. After some time, Bruce commanded his body of highlanders to by-pass the main battle, and due to the fact that they were lightly armed, they climbed the steep rock-faces nearby to take the enemy in the rear. They reached the top to be confronted by a body of English knights. They immediately launched into what in

Rievaulx Abbey

later years became known as a 'highland charge', ie, no real tactics other than violent brute force, running straight in, yelling, with swords drawn, slashing at everything in sight. It certainly worked, the knights scattering before its fury. The Scalachronica says that they ran like hares before a hound. With the highlanders attacking the hilltop defenders from the rear, and with renewed efforts from the Scots below under Douglas and Randolph, the English resistance collapsed.

Bruce then sent Walter Stewart off with 500 horsemen at the

gallop to capture the English King. Unfortunately, Edward was warned just in time and escaped from Rievaulx. Legend states that he had no time to grab any possessions, and had to make his get-away in his nightshirt. Stewart and his horsemen chased him all the way to York, but he found safety behind its gates and walls. The Scots had to be content with the capture of all the King of England's personal belongings left behind at Rievaulx.

The battle came to be called the Battle of Byland, due to the fact that the initial fight took place in the vicinity of what was known as Old Byland. Compared to Stirling Bridge or Bannock-burn, Byland is little remembered, and although it was not as deci-sive as Bannockburn, it was surely more of an embarrassment to the English. After all, their king was defeated and had to make an ignominious retreat deep within his own kingdom, and his army was scattered although it had had the obvious advantage where choice of ground was concerned.

Not very far from Old Byland stands Byland Abbey which is sometimes mistaken by people for Rievaulx. Rievaulx today is an imposing ruin. It stands a little west of the B1257, north-west of the village of Helmsley.

After their victory, the Scots struck east towards the coast. At Beverley, just north of Hull, they took what they could from the area. York was too tough a nut to crack without siege engines, although it was now on the English front line, the Scots striking ever further south.

Bruce had recently raided as far south as Preston on the west. The Scots had been delighted to discover the resources of iron when they arrived in Barrow-in-Furness, and quickly shipped it north for the construction of weaponry, as iron was scarce in Scotland.

Although in his pig-headedness Edward II was still not willing to concede Scotland's rights, matters on the dynastic front were improving for Bruce. His marriage produced another three children. Queen Elizabeth had a girl, Margaret, and then a son, David, who was born on 5 March, 1324 and was later to inherit the throne. A second boy, John, was born in 1326, but unfortunately did not survive.

A bitter blow came with the death of Walter Stewart on 9 April 1326. He would still have been a young man, perhaps only about thirty. He contracted some illness when staying in Bathgate, and wasted away. In Barbour's words:

His illness waxed aye more and more
Till, from the aspect that he wore
Men saw that he was due to pay
The debt from which no creature may...
Escape.

Bruce would never know what effect Walter would have on the future monarchy of Scotland. He had fought tirelessly for Bruce's cause, helping to secure his hold on the throne, and had been rewarded with the hand of the Princess Marjorie. He was the father of the future Robert II of Scotland, but he had witnessed the birth of Bruce's son David, and would think that the crown would pass down through a Bruce dynasty.

Walter had been granted lands in the Bathgate area as part of Marjorie's dowry, and he must have had a residence of some sort in the vicinity. When he died, his body was taken west to be buried in Paisley Abbey beside his wife.

Around the end of 1326, unrest broke out in England which was eventually to lead to civil war. King Edward's queen, Isabel, had taken a lover, Mortimer. The gathered to their support the many disenchanted lords in England, using Edward, Prince of Wales, as their figurehead.

The Prince of Wales was fifteen years old. Queen Isabel, acting as regent for her son, called a parliament for 24 January 1327, which met at Westminster Hall, the oldest part of the Palace of Westminster. What took place was merely a formality. Edward II was deposed and his son was proclaimed Edward III of England. He was crowned on 1 February 1327. His father was captured and imprisoned, first in Kenilworth Castle, then Berkeley Castle. He escaped from Berkeley, but was recaptured, and Queen Isabel plotted his murder to prevent his escaping again and rallying support for his cause.

He was held down and a marrow bone was inserted into his rectum. A red hot poker was then inserted through the bone to kill him, leaving no visible wound to arouse suspicions. It was said that his screams could be heard for miles. The room in Berkeley Castle when this horror took place on 21 September 1327 still exists, and the castle is open to the public.

Edward II was buried in Gloucester Cathedral, where his impressive alabaster tomb still stands. He is depicted in repose, the marvellous effigy showing him with flowing locks and beard, a picture of serenity.

The first confrontation of the new reign in England came when Bruce became tired of the depradations of English pirates on Scots' shipping. Many Scots had been captured and clapped into irons simply for being Scots, and Bruce moved troops towards the border, ready to retaliate.

This was Edward III's chance for glory. He raised a huge army, and marched north.

CHAPTER 11

The Final Acts of War

TO COUNTER EDWARD III'S aggressive stance, Bruce sent Douglas and Randolph south, while he himself is thought to have crossed to Ireland, possibly to organise shipments of arms and food and to negotiate with the Anglo-Irish lords.

Douglas and Randolph crossed the Kielder Gap, a well-used border pass, and followed the valley of the north Tyne to where rich pickings could be gleaned in the flat countryside running towards Durham.

Edward III's huge army had an extra weapon at its disposal – 2,500 heavy cavalry. These were Hainaulters, crack European troops riding heavy warhorses. They had been hired for £14,000, a vast sum in the 14th century, and were to be used to crush the Scots horsemen once and for all. One of the Hainaulters was Jean le Bel, who wrote a chronicle in later life, giving us an eye-witness account of what happened.

Douglas and Randolph's force, all hobelars, extremely lightly armed and unencumbered by anything that could slow them down, rode south during July 1327. The English army, which as usual outnumbered the Scots two or perhaps three to one, could not match the mobility of the Scots.

The English reached Durham, where they saw great plumes of smoke staining the horizon, and realised this was the result of the burning of crops and villages by Douglas and Randolph's men. They turned west in pursuit, and after two days of marching they arrived in the area of Blanchland Abbey, but although scenes of devastation marked their route, none of the Scots could be found. The Scots had actually swung south, crossing Weardale, and were now ravaging the valley of the River Gaunless. (Barbour calls it Cockdale in his narrative, but this area was originally the parish of Cockfield – hence the confusion. There is still a village named Cockfield in the Gaunless area.)

The English had no idea where the Scots had gone, which shows how difficult communication was in those days. All information was by word of mouth, and even if the locals had wanted to report the whereabouts of the Scots, they would have no idea where to seek out the main English army in order to pass on this intelligence.

The English commanders decided that the best course of action was to cut off the Scots' line of retreat, and the order was given to march north. They eventually reached Haydon Bridge, a village on the South Tyne, a little west of Hexham. (I remember this place well from the large weir across the river, beside the A69 Carlisle to Newcastle road.) The English settled down to wait, and le Bel, in his chronicle, remembered how their bread was ruined, as it was strapped behind their saddles and had been soaked through with horse sweat. He also recalled the torrential rain that never let up for a whole week, making life in the field unbearable for man and beast. The Scots were inured to this type of weather, and seemed to have seen it as a minor nuisance, whereas the English accounts speak of the blow it was to morale, with the soldiers' and the horses' leathers starting to rot with the damp, weapons rusting, and the misery of sleeping in the damp conditions.

Edward III began to despair. He promised a knighthood and a grant of land to anyone who could tell him the whereabouts of the Scots so that his army could bring them to battle. Various English squires galloped off to try and win this prize. One of them, Thomas Rokeby, was lucky or unlucky enough to discover the Scots by riding into them, and he was captured. When questioned by Douglas, Rokeby told him of King Edward's promise, and Douglas let him go to claim his prize, saying that the Scots would be waiting for the enemy at Stanhope in Weardale. When word reached Edward's army at Haydon Bridge, there was great delight – the Scots would be brought to battle at last. (MAP B8)

The rivers were running high after the rain, so the English marched a little west, crossed the South Tyne at Haltwhistle and headed south down Allendale, following the line of the B6295, towards the infant River Wear. This part of Northumberland is bleak moorland, which must have been dreadful to cross in driving rain in 1327. Walking it today, I have tried to imagine what the great lords of southern England thought of the landscape, quite apart from the Hainault cavalrymen. They reached the Wear at the Cowshill area, and followed the river downstream, along the line of the modern A689.

It has been debated at length over the years where the various confrontations between the two armies took place, even on which side of the river either side was based. No-one locally has any knowledge of this, and there are no place names either to give any clues.

The Scots probably held the hillside directly opposite Stanhope, just far enough back to be out of bowshot, with the Wear running across the base of the slope. The Wear at this point is not much of a barrier to anyone determined to cross. The hillside gives a view northwards over the route of the B6728, and as most modern country roads follow the line of old trails, the Scots may have expected the English to take this route south. Unfortunately, there have been open cast mine workings on the hillside, with later tree planting to cover the scarring, so it is difficult to imagine positioning today.

The English most likely camped on the flatland below, where there is now a football pitch just south of the railway track.

The English sent a squad of archers round to try and take the Scots in the rear, but Douglas was wise to their plan, hiding a body of horsemen ready to attack them, while he himself rode out alone to act as decoy and hopefully lure them to where the Scots' horsemen could attack. Unfortunately, he was recognised by one of the enemy who shouted to his fellows that it was Douglas and they all immediately took flight, knowing that some ploy must be afoot.

Edward then sent a herald over to the Scots to say that the

English army would pull back a little so that the Scots could come across the river to the flat ground where battle could be joined, or the Scots should allow the English to cross, the same rules applying. The Scots replied that they were in the realm of England, they had burned it and wasted it, and were quite happy where they were.

The English set up their tents for the night, but they got very little sleep. At irregular intervals the Scottish army would let out a roar with horns blowing, as if they were charging in the dark. Le Bel reported, 'it seemed the biggest devils in hell were there to destroy us'. The following day the English made a feint to cross the river, but that was all that happened, other than hot-heads on both sides skirmishing by the river banks. The Scots were impressed by two sights they had never seen before. The English had brought cannon with them, although the rain had rendered them unusable, and the English knights were wearing wooden emblems on top of their helmets – eagles, lions, etc – which were the latest fashion. The Scots admired these, so much so that the fact was mentioned in records.

That night the Scots struck camp and moved upstream some two miles to Stanhope Park, an old hunting ground, but they left their fires burning. At first light the English discovered that the Scots' positions were deserted, and when it was realised the Scots had moved upstream, they also struck camp and re-settled opposite the Scots in a similar situation to the first arrangement, although if anything, the Scots were now in a stronger position. Standing on the hillside which was the site of the Scots' original position and looking up the valley, it would seem obvious that they would have moved to the steep hill jutting out slightly which stands on the south side of the river at Eastgate. This is theory, but I feel in my bones that this is the spot, and I can visualise the English moving to the flatlands where a giant silver chimney now stands on the opposite side of the river.

The next night, 4 August 1327, Douglas decided that it was time to put the fear of death into the enemy. Taking 500 picked horsemen, he moved well away from the two encampments, then forded the river, to come upon the rear of the enemy camp. The troop was spotted by some Englishmen, but Douglas shouted back in an English accent, 'Is there no watch, by St George?' The enemy, thinking this was perhaps reinforcements, let them trot on. They made their way into the English camp, then suddenly the cry went up 'Douglas! Douglas! You shall all die, lords of England'. The 500 Scots' horsemen went forward at the gallop, slashing at tent ropes, stabbing down with spears.

Douglas threw himself at Edward of England's tent, actually slaying Edward's personal chaplain, but he could hear that the initial shock of the attack was wearing off. He had to get the Scots regrouped and away to safety, so he abandoned the attack on the English king and blew his horn to give the signal for retreat. Douglas sat astride his horse at the riverside, making sure his men were crossing safely. As the last man passed, an Englishman suddenly ran from hiding and struck Douglas with a club, stunning him. Luckily Douglas was able to slay his assailant and get across the river, his head spinning. When the Scots returned to camp, Randolph remarked that perhaps they should all have gone over on this night attack, but Douglas had taken only the risk he thought appropriate. Later it was discovered that over 300 Englishmen had been slain.

The next day, the Scots announced that they were going to attack the English camp again the following night. Having had a real fright, with their king a hairsbreadth from capture, the English took this threat seriously. They knew that if they could bring the Scots to battle – which would assuredly happen – they would annihilate them with their superiority in numbers. The English needed a battle, deep inside their own realm, but the Scots had nothing to lose by using subterfuge instead.

That night they stoked up their fires and left a few trumpeters and men to create an illusion of activity. In the darkness the Scots started to file away south over the bogland at their rear, jettisoning any surplus equipment. Bundles of wood were used to fill ditches, allowing the hobins to cross burns and pools. Once clear, they swung north-west, and at a quicker pace made for the border.

In the morning, as the sun rose, the realisation dawned on the English that the Scots had gone. Scouts were sent out, but when the Scots were nowhere to be found and it was evident that they had headed for home, Edward III broke down in tears of frustration. There was nothing he could do but disband the army and head south. The Hainaulters had still to be paid their £14,000, which they would need. Their fine horses were shadows of their former selves after the rain, the moorland treks and the lack of food trying to outface the Scots. The expense was a disaster to the English exchequer.

What had happened was also a terrible loss of face. The Scots had proved that they could ravage England unopposed and be more than a match tactically for the English, almost capturing their king in the process. At last the English began to think very carefully about the situation regarding Scotland.

Bruce decided to press the advantage personally. No sooner had Douglas and Randolph returned to Scotland to give a report on what became known as the Weardale Campaign, than Bruce told them they were immediately returning to England. He had decided to make it look as if the Scots were intending to annexe Northumberland. Bruce knew well what a hateful thing it was to encroach on another country, but after so many years trying to get the English to recognise the nation of Scotland as a separate entity, he had reached exasperation point. The fact that he was not in the best of health must have influenced matters too.

Bruce oversaw the siege of Norham Castle, just south of the Tweed, the ruins of which today give us a glimpse of its former strength. During September 1327, Douglas began to besiege Alnwick, and Randolph to besiege Warkworth. The whole of Northumberland was ravaged and terrorised.

One day as Bruce was attending to business at Norham, a party approached under a flag of truce. He must have thought, 'What now?' It was an English delegation, come to negotiate for peace, for recognition of his kingship and of Scotland as a nation state. It was as welcome as it was unexpected.

Thirty-one years earlier Edward Longshanks had begun the war against Scotland from Norham Castle. In a twist of fate, Bruce was besieging Norham when the English finally came to their senses, realising that the war against Scotland was futile.

Norham Castle

Norham, which is under the care of English Heritage, is well worth a visit. A place for some reflection, it stands just north of the A698, on the south bank of the Tweed, midway between Coldstream and Berwick.

Bruce had no sooner left Norham Castle and returned to Scotland to start compiling the legislation for the peace treaty, when news was brought to him that his queen, Elizabeth, was dead. Elizabeth had gone on a pilgrimage to St Duthac's Sanctuary at Tain in Easter Ross. This journey was no doubt connected with the fact that it was in this sanctuary that Elizabeth, along with others of Bruce's womenfolk, was taken and held, before being kept in English prisons for many years. Perhaps she had made a vow that if she ever gained her freedom, she would one day go back.

On her return journey from the pilgrimage, she was travelling along the northern coast of Banff where, legend states, she fell from her horse, suffering internal bleeding. She had never fully recovered from complications during the birth of her second son who did not survive. She was taken to the castle of Cullen, where she died on 26 October 1327. In preparation for the conveyance of her body south to her last resting place at Dunfermline Abbey, she was disembowelled and her body embalmed. Her entrails were buried in the Lady Chapel at the Church of Cullen. (MAP A3)

Cullen was the final place I visited before I started to write this

The Church at Cullen

book. I was really lucky on this occasion. It took me a while to locate the old church dedicated to St Mary, as it stands slightly south-west of the town, near Cullen House, the seat of the Earl of Seafield. As I pulled up on my motorcycle, an elderly couple, obviously caretakers, were just locking up, and when I explained why I was there, they unlocked the door and allowed me to take photographs of the interior. Elizabeth's entrails had been interred in the 'Lady Chapel'. The Lady Chapel dedicated to the Virgin Mary was usually located to the east of the high altar.

The interior of the church has changed greatly since 1327, but a church has existed here in one form or another since 1236. There are two later knights' tombs within the building, one from 1404, the other from 1554, both very impressive. What really took my eye were the wooden stalls and galleries dated 1602, quartered with the arms of Douglas which has Bruce's heart as part of its make-up. The building is an absolute jewel, and is worth examining even from the exterior, if you are not as lucky as I was in gaining access.

I believe the building where Elizabeth actually died is contained within, or was close to the present Cullen House, which is partially visible from the churchyard of St Mary's. There has been a fortified building here for many centuries, and it was the Earl of Seafield who remarked laconically at the act of Union in 1707, 'There's an end to an auld sang!' We'll see – we Scots have hung on pretty well so far.

There is a 'Castlehill' in Cullen by the viaduct at the seafront. This mound is surmounted by a little domed structure on pillars. There is no doubt that a castle of sorts once stood here, although Cullen House is most likely the site of Elizabeth's death.

Bruce had married Elizabeth, not for some dynastic advancement, but for love, and after her death he endowed a chantry priest at

St Mary's, Cullen, to pray for her soul. She had at least lived long enough to see the offer of a final peace, even if she never saw the conclusion of her husband's life work.

On 30 October 1327, negotiations began at Newcastle to hammer out the final peace treaty. The terms offered by the Scottish side of the delegation appear incredibly magnanimous, but all Bruce had ever desired was recognition of Scotland's sovereignty. The final peace was signed the following year, a year before Bruce's death, and became known as the Treaty of Edinburgh. It was concluded on 17 March 1328, and was signed within the monastery of Holyrood, with Bruce lying on his sickbed.

The ruins of this building stand adjacent to the Palace of Holyroodhouse at the bottom of the Royal Mile in Edinburgh. It is perhaps fitting that at the time of writing, Scotland's new parliament building is being constructed at Holyrood (although public opinion was mostly against this site – somewhere more eye-catching and forward-looking being most people's prerogative).

Bishop Lamberton lived just long enough to see the culmination of everything he had strived for. He had backed Wallace, then Bruce, always with the dream of seeing his country free. He died shortly after the Treaty was completed and is most likely buried somewhere in the ruins of his beloved cathedral of St Andrews.

The peace with England, of course, did nothing to divert them from trying to subjugate Scotland for the next three hundred years. But it did mean that they had no validity for their actions. In the Treaty of Edinburgh they had recognised Scotland as a separate entity, free for all time from English domination, so at least they could not use the 'Lord Paramount of Scotland' argument ever again.

Even though England far outstrips Scotland in terms of monetary wealth and population, all the English have ever managed to wrest from the Scots was Berwick-on-Tweed and overlordship of the Isle of Man, which had been a bone of contention for a long time before Bruce.

It makes me proud that my ancestors managed to hold off

tyranny so well; after all, the blood that runs in my veins is the blood of men who fought alongside Bruce, and not only Bruce. Many generations of my ancestors stood time and time again against aggressive inroads from the south. I can take pride in that. I only need to see the people of Scotland take pride too, to make the picture complete.

CHAPTER 12

The Death of the Bruce

DURING HIS FINAL YEARS, Bruce enjoyed some relief from the rigours of life he had gone through, constantly living life in the field, fulfilling his role not only as king, but as soldier and general too, more often than not roughing it under the stars. This had taken its toll.

For his enjoyment he had had a house constructed, not a fortified dwelling, but a manor, from which he could hunt, sail and enjoy family life. It was a pleasant place, with thatched roofs, the king's chamber having glazed windows and plastered and painted walls.

The manor stood just north of Dumbarton, halfway between the town and the flyover of the modern A82, on the west bank of the River Leven which flows from Loch Lomond to the Clyde. Its site was later replaced by Mains of Cardross farm, which has since been demolished. The name 'Mains' is a recent corruption of 'demense', or lord's manor. (MAP C31)

From there Bruce could sail round his beloved west coast in one of the ships he kept at his disposal. There is a record of one boat being hauled for repair into the tiny burn that flows into the Leven. This burn is just north of the farm site, running across the fields from Dalmoak a little further west.

There is even a record of some of Bruce's staff. William, Gilchrist and Gilfillan looked after his parks. Gillis hunted for game for the royal kitchens.

Having visited the site several times, one feature always intrigues me. The edges of the surrounding fields have raised dykes, or earthen walls. These are obviously old as there are some quite large trees growing on them. Could these be the boundaries of Bruce's parks or gardens?

You can reach the site of Bruce's house by taking the footpath

up the west bank of the Leven from Dumbarton, or by taking the
A812 north out of Dumbarton and parking in the Dalmoak vicinity.
There is a railway track to the east, but there is a little farm access
tunnel that can be used to reach the fields and the house site beyond.

I have stood on the ramparts of Dumbarton Castle, a little to
the south, and looked out over the site, thinking of Bruce spend-
ing his final years in this area. I realised that I was standing in that part of the castle named Wallace's Prison,
supposedly where Wallace was kept for his

final days before his transfer to London and his   Whithorn Priory
dreadful death.

There is a long-standing local tradition that Bruce's house
stood in the suburb of Dumbarton called Castlehill, but this is
incorrect.

At the very end of his life, Bruce undertook a pilgrimage to
Whithorn in Galloway to visit the shrine of St Ninian. St Ninian
is believed to have introduced Christianity into Scotland during
the 4th century. Bruce was evidently in pain during this journey;
this we can gather from the time it took to complete the trip. He
was in Girvan on 6 February 1329, then moved on to Lochinch
where he had to rest for a month. He next travelled to Glenluce
and Monreith, and reached Whithorn on 1 April. He remained
there for four days, praying to the saint. (MAP C17)

When I last visited Whithorn. I drove down the M74, cutting
across to Dumfries to photograph the plaque in the town centre
which commemorates Bruce's murder of the Red Comyn, before
enjoying the bike ride right along the Solway Coast to Whithorn.

There are extensive ruins at Whithorn, many dating back to the 12th century. You can wander through the remains of the priory church and various old vaults. Several rooms contain artefacts discovered from the many excavations that have been carried out.

Doorway at Whithorn

It is worth visiting the Isle of Whithorn nearby, a little village clustered around its old tower house. Pilgrims landed here from various countries to visit the shrine of St Ninian inland. Just east of the village is a ruined chapel dating from the 13th century. A cairn stands in the village for making promises. You make your promise then add a stone to the pile.

I remember on the drive back north up the Ayrshire coast, I glanced across to the lighthouse that marks the ruins of Turnberry Castle, and realised that Bruce must have passed here on his final journey. I imagined him looking out at the view, remembering his boyhood forays in the district, and thinking of all that had transpired since those days. He would have recalled his games with his brothers, every one of whom had predeceased him, and I hope that he realised that all his heartache, all his loss, was worth it.

He would probably despair if he could imagine what has happened to Scotland since these times, but it is the memory of people like himself, embedded within us as a nation, which has put into gear the chain of events that will follow the 'yes' vote for the restoration of a Scottish parliament, which took place on 11 September 1997.

When Bruce was back at the manor in Cardross, he confessed to his friends and advisors that he had made a vow as a young knight that if he could free Scotland from the English yoke, he would go on a crusade to the Holy Land. As peace and liberation had come only at the end of his life, he could not personally make this crusade, but as he had made the vow, he wished it to be honoured. He explained that he knew his death was approaching, and when he died, he wanted his heart to be removed and taken on a journey to the Holy Land, to be presented at the Holy Sepulchre in Jerusalem and then returned and buried within Melrose Abbey, a place he obviously felt much affection for, as he had contributed to its rebuilding after it had been sacked by the English.

Bruce asked his friends to choose a warrior to carry out this, his last wish. With one voice they answered 'Douglas'. Bruce replied that he hoped this was what they would say. Douglas was brought before his King in tears. This terror of brave knights, whose name alone was enough to turn the tide of a battle, despaired at the loss of his friend, the man whose cause he had dedicated his life to.

Robert the Bruce, the first knight of Christendom, hero-King of Scots, died on 7 June 1329. He was fifty-four years and eleven months old.

Barbour said:-

And when folk heard that he was dead
From home to home the sorrow spread
Then might one see men tear their hair
And wring their hands in deep despair
And knights were seen to weep full sore
And madly rend the clothes they wore
Lamenting for his nobleness
His wisdom, honour, manliness
Above all for his company
That he bestowed so courteously.

Bruce's body was embalmed and carried across Scotland to Dunfermline. It was taken by the south end of Loch Lomond, probably then by Fintry, and down the Carron Valley to the first night's halt at Dunipace, where Wallace had been raised by his uncle, formerly the priest there. (MAP C34) The next night his body lay in the abbey at Cambuskenneth, close to the scene of his great victory at Bannockburn, then he was carried to his final resting place in Dunfermline Abbey to rest beside the body of Elizabeth, his queen. His heart had been removed and encased in a casket of silver, and Douglas was already preparing for their last great adventure together.

Bruce's tomb had been commissioned well in advance of his death, and its magnificence was fitting for the hero-King. (MAP A14)

It was constructed from marble and designed by Thomas de Chatres, a famous stoneworker, who created it in his Paris studio. The sum of £12, 10s (£12.50p) was paid from the Scots exchequer for its carriage through Bruges and England to Dunfermline. The mason who erected it in Dunfermline Abbey received £38, 2s, and an iron railing to surround it cost £12, 8s, 2d. Robert of Lessunden, who was responsible for erecting the railing, was also given the gift of a robe worth £1. John of Linlithgow decorated all the iron work on the tomb with 1100 books of gold leaf which had been purchased in York. A temporary chapel constructed from Baltic timber was set up over the tomb on the day of the funeral. The wax bought to make candles for the ceremony weighed 562st 5lbs.

Dunfermline Abbey

When the tomb was finished it must have been a work of great beauty. But it did not stand alone. Several other monarchs and their queens and several princes and princesses had already been buried at Dunfermline, and their tombs would have been quite a sight. Although Edward Longshanks had fired the Abbey some years before, most of the stonework survived.

You would imagine that the last resting-place of Bruce would be defended to the death by any Scotsman or woman worth their salt. As long as Scotland existed you would expect it to be held in reverence, and protected with vigilance while the merest glimmer of the flame of national pride burned in a Scottish heart. But it was not to be.

On 28 March 1560, Dunfermline Abbey was razed by the

Reformers. Armed with hammers and axes, they were determined to destroy everything they thought smacked of idolatry, and Bruce's tomb, along with every other, was smashed to pieces and the church destroyed. Four years later, the nave was cleared of the debris and refitted for use as the parish church. But the story does not end there.

On 28 July 1807, a search was instigated in the ruins of the Abbey for the tombs of the kings and this was recorded by Mr John Graham Dalyell. At this time, in the eastern half of the ruins, six large stones could be seen lying together in two rows of three. The middle stone of the west row, being the largest, was lifted with some difficulty. About 5ft of earth containing bone fragments was removed, then a stone coffin was found containing a complete skeleton. This coffin was not directly under the covering stone; only one half was directly underneath, with the other half of the coffin protruding to the west. The searchers then put as much as they could of the stone coffin back in place, replaced some of the earth on top and then the large covering stone. It must have been quite a difficult task as this cover was 10ft long, 5ft broad, and about 8in thick. At a later date, when rain had washed through some of the pile of earth that had been removed, a leaden plate was discovered with a lion engraved on it, surrounded by the legend 'Robertus Dei Gratia Rex Scotorum' (Robert, by God's Grace, King of Scots). This plate was taken by the Earl of Elgin, a descendant of Robert the Bruce, and presumably is still in his family's possession. The present site of these stones appears to be within the little northern projection of the church, facing towards the Abbot's house, which at the time of writing is the Abbey shop. It is assumed that this is the burial place of most of the royalty interred within the Abbey. Although today this area is contained within the north-projecting transept, in medieval times it was within the main body of the church. The walls of the present church do not follow exactly the lines of the original.

The next information on Bruce's tomb I found in a report written in February 1818, just before the discovery of the tomb:

Several years ago, a monument had been erected to the memory of the late Earl of Elgin (who died in 1771) and which, upon its interfering with the plan of the new church, was by the orders of the present Earl, removed to another part of the church yard, and the workmen, in the course of their operations, came upon a stone vault.

In this, I was told the remains of a human skeleton were found, and it has even been asserted that it was ascertained to be that of a female. I am inclined to think it contained the remains of King Robert's Queen, but the skeleton was removed from the place before I had an opportunity of seeing it.

This skeleton was also removed by the Earl of Elgin.

I have come across one other mention of the discovery of Queen Elizabeth's tomb, author unknown. It runs as follows:

A monument erected to the memory of the Earl of Elgin and Kincardine, who died in 1771, had to be removed when the new church was built, and a stone vault was discovered, in which lay the skeleton of a lady, with long hair. It is most likely that this was the body of Queen Elizabeth, the second wife of Robert the Bruce.

Bruce's last resting place came to light when the building plans were being drawn up to construct the church which stands today connected to the western half of the remains from earlier times. The architect, Mr Burn, wished to make a ground plan of the lines of the original walls so that the new building would incorporate all the sites of possible royal tombs. On 17 February 1818, during the progress of these operations, workmen accidentally discovered a vault which lay in the very centre of the ancient cathedral.

It was covered by two stones, the smaller above the head, which lay to the west, and the larger over the body. The stone above the head was complete, but the larger one over the body was broken into several pieces, probably caused by the ruins of the cathedral falling on it. The larger stone was fitted with iron rings as handles, and as the workmen removed the pieces, a body was found beneath, enclosed in lead, with a much decayed cloth covering it. There was a gap in the lead at the feet, and at one of the knees, where the skeleton could be seen within. On top of the covering of lead over the head, another piece of lead had been fashioned into a crown. Luckily, the architect was present, and immediately ordered the tomb to be re-covered, and a watch kept until it could be firmly secured with iron bars. At the same time, arrangements were made for extra security on the other six slabs which were mentioned during the earlier dig of 1807.

It was decided that the tomb should remain secured until the building work on the new church was in an advanced state, whereupon it would be re-opened in the presence of The King's Remembrancer, Henry Jardine, who would record the official report. This duly took place on 5 November 1819, and the information that follows comes from his report.

He recorded that once the covering stones had been removed, Bruce's tomb was 'seven feet long, twenty-two and a half inches in breadth, and eighteen inches deep'. It was completely paved with regularly-cut, smooth stones, each about a foot square, although there was a large fracture across the floor. This tomb sat inside a larger vault, but much of the stonework of this had deteriorated.

Unfortunately, the lead covering had decayed since the original discovery. There were several holes in the lead, and there was much debris in the bottom of the tomb, which on examination turned out to be the sodden oak remains of the coffin. The leaden crown was gone – it must have been stolen by a bystander when the tomb was first discovered.

One side of the tomb was demolished in order to slide a thin board under Bruce's body. Once this was done, it was lifted entirely out of the vault for inspection. The lead covering was found to be crushed in places, and this, coupled with the broken vault covering, makes me think this must have happened when the tomb and church were smashed at the Reformation. The lead covering was stripped back, and it was noticed that there were still some remains of tendons on the skeleton. The skull was removed for the purpose of creating a plaster cast and this was carried out by a Mr Scoular. It was remarked that Bruce had at some time suffered quite a severe fracture of the jaw, probably during one of his adventures in the early part of his reign. The skeleton was measured, and it was decreed that Bruce had stood between 5ft 11ins and 6ft tall.

The Remembrancer goes on to add:

> But the most remarkable circumstance which we observed, upon examining the skeleton, was the state of the sternum, which we found had been sawed asunder longitudinally from top to bottom.

This is obviously from the operation to remove the heart, so Douglas could carry out his last commission.

The decayed cloth that had been thrown over the lead as a shroud contained many threads of gold. It turned out to be toile d'or, or cloth of gold, and a few samples were taken and placed between glass slides.

All who attended the examination of the tomb said that there had been a very rapid decay of the remains since the tomb had first been uncovered.

A large leaden coffin was brought into the church, and four inches of melted pitch were poured into the bottom into which were inserted various leaden boxes containing a copy of Barbour's *Life of Bruce*, several other history books, newspapers of the day, and seven gold and nine silver coins of King George III. (I'm sure Bruce would have loved that!). The board, with Bruce's body lying upon it, was then laid across the top of the lead coffin.

For a while after this the public were allowed access to the new abbey buildings to file past Bruce's remains. As word spread about the discovery of his body, there was a large upsurge in national feeling across Scotland; after all, the 1820 uprising was only a year away.

Some time was spent clearing the site of Bruce's tomb, and during these excavations other artefacts came to light. Broken pieces of black and white marble were found which were obviously remnants of Thomas de Chatre's original memorial. A copper plate 5½in by 4in was found bearing the inscription 'Robertus Scotorum Rex', and it was thought that this plate had originally been attached to the front of the coffin. Later a letter came to light, written by a Dunfermline craftsman, who claimed that he had forged this plate, copying the style of writing from coins of Bruce's time. A stone found with a head carved on it, although badly worn, was assumed to be a likeness of Bruce as it resembles the portraits found on his coins.

All these finds were given to the Museum of Antiquities in Edinburgh, along with some fragments of bone from Bruce's skeleton.

Some 11ft from the spot where Bruce's coffin was discovered, a small leaden box was found. When it was opened, it was found to contain a substance which was probably the bowels of a historical figure. For some reason it was decided that when Bruce's body was re-interred, this box (2ft 6in by 9in by 5in) would be put in beside it.

A new tomb was constructed on the site of the original, and once the brick floor was finished, Bruce's skeleton was placed into the new leaden coffin (as far as I can ascertain, the original lead covering was put back on) and it was filled almost to the top with molten pitch. A leaden lid was soldered on with raised letters which stated:

King Robert Bruce

1329

1819

1329 was the date of the original burial and the re-interment took place in 1819.

The coffin was bricked over with an arch, then a stone covering, 18ins thick, was built around that.

Due to these discoveries, the architect had the plans changed to have 'King Robert the Bruce' inserted into the sides of the top of the steeple in 4ft high letters. The site of Bruce's tomb, now directly under the pulpit of the modern church, was marked by a monumental brass plaque inlaid in the floor above the tomb in 1889 where it can still be seen today.

Dunfermline Abbey is open to visitors during the summer months. The West Window in the old Norman nave was designed by Noel Paton, a 19th-century patriotic artist, and features likenesses of Wallace standing guard over a young woman representing 'Scotia', Malcolm Canmore, St Margaret, and Bruce.

There is a cast of Bruce's skull in a case within the Abbey. There is also one in the Museum of Scotland in Edinburgh, and several others are to be found around the country. I always notice the two crossed bottom teeth when I look at the cast, and see a bit of the real Bruce. People must have noticed this in his lifetime, and it brings a smile to my face to see it nearly 700 years on.

The 'Liberator' Exhibition in the Smith Art Gallery in Stirling in 1997 had a small fragment of Bruce's coffin on show in one of the cases. It was on loan from a private individual.

I have done my best to bring the story of Bruce to the present day, but there is one side of him that I cannot cover, and that is what Bruce really looked like. Barbour gives descriptions of some individuals in his epic poem but unfortunately does not mention Bruce. One or two people have made reconstructions from skull casts, but these are not conclusive evidence. There is a brief passage in John Mair's *Historia Majoris Britanniae* which may have been repeating authentic tradition when it states:

> His figure was graceful and athletic, with broad shoulders, his features were handsome, he had the yellow hair of the northern race, with blue and sparkling eyes. His intellect was quick, and he had the gift of fluent speech in the vernacular, delightful to listen to.

Postscript

Sir James – El Bueno Peregrino

WHEN DOUGLAS SET OUT ON his last commission, he probably sailed from Berwick. (Some sources say he left from Montrose, but Berwick seems more likely.) He was accompanied by a body of picked knights and men-at-arms, all experienced fighters, proven in the field after the many years of conflict with England.

Only a few of his companions' names have come down to us – William and John Sinclair of Roslin, William Keith of Galston and Robert and Walter Logan.

I can see Douglas aboard the ship, sitting in his cabin, eyeing the silver casket on the table before him containing the heart of the Bruce.

They first docked at Sluys, where visitors remarked on the magnificence that Douglas displayed, not only by the warlike appearance of his company, but by the quality of belongings seen aboard ship. From here, the Scots followed the coastline round northern Spain, evidently pausing at Santander.

In I.M. Davis's book on Douglas, mention is made of a reference from the Calendar of Documents Relating to Scotland, where a stone is mentioned near Santander which was pointed out as a memorial of 'a great warrior called El Douglas who came long ago to fight the infidels in Spain'. I wonder if this stone still exists? It is always something to look forward to discovering, at a later date. One wee detail I like is the fact that the Spanish call Douglas Du-glas, the same pronunciation as the Gaelic.

The Scots then sailed down the coast of Portugal, and knowing that the Moors were trying to increase their hold on Europe, they sailed up the Guadalquivir to Seville, to offer their services to Alfonso XI of Castile who was based there, ready to continue his fight against the Moorish forces.

Douglas was one of the most famous men in Europe, and

word of his arrival soon spread around the Christian army. Many knights flocked to have a look at this noted soldier, many of them English, who were understandably excited to have a chance fighting with Douglas for once, instead of in opposition.

When Douglas appeared, shock travelled through the watchers due to the fact that he bore no scars upon his face. Many knights, their faces carved by many years spent on European battlefields, found it difficult to believe that this was indeed the famous Douglas. Douglas remarked, 'I have always had strong hands to protect my face'.

The Scots were absorbed into Alfonso's forces, Douglas being put in charge of a section of the army, but accounts differ as to the size of the force under his command. An advance was made eastwards, the main Moorish forces being based around Granada, some 200 miles away.

The Moors had taken control of the Castillo della Estrella (The Castle of the Stars), a strategic fortress sitting midway between Seville and Granada, close to the village of Teba, and it was decided to besiege this fortress. The Christian army, including Douglas's men, dug in, but a Moorish

Castle of the Stars

army led by Osmin, an experienced soldier, came to the castle's relief. They based themselves at Turron, several miles away on the far side of the Rio Guadalteba, which flows a mile or so from the castle.

Osmin tried to attack the army of Alfonso by stratagem. He sent one arm of his force directly towards the Castillo della Estrella as a diversion, while his main force circled around to attack the Christian camp. Alsfonso realised what was afoot, and sent an arm of his own force down to contest the river crossing. This party included Douglas, wearing Bruce's heart in the casket about his neck. Alfonso kept back the main part of his army to counter the Moorish threat to his camp.

Down at the riverside, Douglas and his men charged deep into the enemy ranks, perhaps misunderstanding the battle commands issued by foreign commanders. Realising his mistake, Douglas called on the Scots to close round him, ready to fight their way back to the main body of the Christian army. Fighting furiously through the Moors in front, Douglas saw that William Sinclair of Roslin was isolated and threatened by a group of the enemy. Douglas reigned his horse round and galloped to his friend's aid, more Moors closing in on every side.

Meanwhile, Osmin's army discovered that the Christian camp was stoutly defended and had to withdraw, their tactics having failed on this occasion.

After the Moors had left the battlefield, William Keith of Galston, who had broken an arm during an assault on the castle and therefore had not taken part in Douglas's attack, searched the field with the remaining Scots looking for Douglas. They discovered his body, with five deep wounds, surrounded by the bodies of many of the enemy, and at this they lamented like men gone mad, much to the astonishment of the Spanish host. On lifting Douglas's body, they found the silver casket containing Bruce's heart beneath him.

The castle at Teba fell to the Christian army a few days later, so we can at least say Douglas's final fight was a victory. The Scots would not bury Douglas in a far-off land, so remote from his beloved Scotland. His heart was removed and his body was boiled in a cauldron till the flesh parted from the bones, and was buried nearby in holy ground. His skeleton was borne back to Scotland, and his heart acted companion to that of Bruce.

The greatest fiction writer would be hard put to pen a story as complex and inspiring as that of Bruce and Douglas – how Bruce saved him as a lad, how Douglas pledged himself to Scotland and Bruce at the Arrickstone, and how Douglas had died carrying his friend's heart after several lifetimes' worth of adventuring between them.

Bruce's heart was taken to Melrose Abbey, that jewel of the borderland, and buried there. Douglas's bones and heart were returned to the village that bore his name and interred in the church of St Bride, where in later years, his bastard son, Archie the Grim, would erect a fitting tomb above his remains. (Isn't Archie the Grim a great name? It wasn't because he was grumpy, it was because of 'his terrible countenance in warfare against the English' – very much his father's son.)

The legend of Douglas throwing Bruce's heart forward into the Moorish army, crying something like 'Go forward, brave heart, and I will follow or die', would seem to be a later invention, even though it is included in some copies of Barbour's work. It was added to Barbour's 1370 original by a later hand.

When I first read the story of Douglas dying on this mission, carrying the heart of Bruce, I vowed that one day I would go and see the place where this happened. I planned trips by motorcycle to Spain, to go and see this epic spot, perhaps getting a ferry from southern England to Santander, where I could enquire about the stone dedicated to El Duglas. In the end, when I discovered the location of Douglas's death, and how close it lay to the Costa del Sol where so many Scots take their holidays, I ended up booking a seat on a charter flight to Malaga in 1997, and hiring a car from there to travel inland.

I had dreamt of going for so long that the trip had an unreal quality to it, but I can remember all the details vividly. I would like to have gone by bike, and perhaps I still shall. It would be nice to be reasonably dry for a change. And it was this thought that made me think of how it must have been for the Scots in 1330. They must have thought, 'How come my armour isn't getting rusty?' and 'What is that yellow ball up there in the sky?'

I knew that the Castle of the Stars stood above a little village called Teba, which is so small by Spanish standards that it is only shown on maps of Andalusia. Teba is roughly 75 kilometres (50 miles) more or less due north of Malaga.

The road north out of Malaga started off as a decent stretch of dual carriageway, but as the coast was left behind it got gradually worse until it was not much more than a dusty track in places, although upgrading was taking place. Used to the power of a big bike, an 850cc car came as a shock, especially overtaking, when I had to shout abuse at the unfortunate vehicle to get it to shift at a reasonable rate, before oncoming trucks impressed their tyre tracks upon me.

The wee Spanish hilltop villages are a delight, and I knew I was nearing Teba when Ardales came into view. Cave paintings have been found in this area, proving how long it has been a centre of population. As I drove downhill to cross the Rio Guadalteba, I caught site of the castle ruins in the distance. I stopped to take in the view. The castle stood white on its craggy hilltop, and I looked at the flat landscape surrounding me – perfect cavalry country. It was quiet, with no other human in sight, when a tortoise crossed the road in front of me. I wondered if there were many about, and imagined Douglas's men spotting one and wondering what on earth it was. Own suit of armour and everything!

The hill with the castle on top was high on the south side facing me, but on its other side it has a shelf about half way up where the village of Teba stands.

Before I explored further, I entered a little bodega for a beer and a snack. It was memorable, as I ate the best chorizo sausage I have ever tasted. I knew there was a monument somewhere in the village to Bruce and Douglas, and I tried to get directions by citing words like 'Roberto Uno' and 'Escocia' at the barman. Eventually his eyes lit up, and he produced a drawing of the village with the monument marked upon it, saying 'Si, El Duglas'.

He gave me the drawing, which I still have.

Monument at Teba

I found the monument at the top of the village. It was placed there in 1988, the funds for it raised by a Douglas Mackintosh, Deputy Attorney of Brockville, Ontario, and his uncle, the Earl of Selkirk. The stone was carved from granite in Scotland, and left on its journey to Spain in August 1988. This block, standing on its plinth, surrounded by an iron chain, has an inscription in English on one side, and Spanish on the other. The English runs as follows:-

Sir James Douglas
most loyal comrade in arms of
Robert the Bruce
King of Scots
While on his way to present the Heart of
Bruce at the Church of the Most
Holy Sepulchre Jerusalem, the good
Sir James turned aside to support
King Alfonso XI capture the
stragetic Castle of the Stars, Teba
and was slain in battle August 25
1330.

The other side, in Spanish, gives a little more information, and runs as follows:

Camino de la Cruzado fallecio Sir James Douglas
lunchardo contra los moros al lado
del rey don Alfonso XI cavo cerca del castillo
della estrella de TEBA el 25 de agosto del
ano 1330. Caballero lealisimo del rey
Roberto 1 de Escocia y adalid opt–
imo en las guerras de independencia. Sir James
el Bueno peregrinaba a la Tierra Santo bajo ju–
ramento de consagrar el corazon real del
libertador de Escocia en el altar de la Iglesia
del Santo Sepulcro en Jerusalem.

Libertador de Escocia – I like the ring that has to it.

As at most monuments in towns all over the world, three or four youths eyed me with open suspicion, obviously giving the

Spanish equivalent of 'What's this idiot all about?' as I took photos from every possible distance and angle.

Their tune soon changed when I opened a bag containing a dozen bottles of 'Black Douglas' beer which I had bought in my local off-sales and dragged all the way with me. The ones I didn't hand out, I left on top of the memorial itself. I actually got a couple of snaps of the local youths holding the bottles aloft, shouting 'El Duglas!'.

From there I went up to the hilltop to explore the castle itself. It still has its central keep, more or less entire, but the remnants of the double row of curtain walling all around the hilltop site left me in no doubt of the strength this place once had.

Even on the south-facing cliff, there were remnants of heavy fortification. Up there, above the village which was laid out like a map below, all was silent. A few semi-wild goats roamed the castle ruins, but they were my only companions. I climbed the tower stairs and looked out of a window over towards the Rio Guadalteba where the Scots had fought and died, just as some Moorish soldier must have done hundreds of years before. Scanning the landscape with a trained eye, I tried to work out where Douglas's last fight had taken place. I noticed a spot that looked likely, where the river banks were particularly low for cavalry to cross, and said to myself 'Well, that's the spot I would have chosen.'

Keeping this site fixed in my mind, I walked the mile or so from the base of the hill to the river side. When I reached the spot, I was more than taken aback to find a great big Scottish-looking thistle right on the site I had pinpointed from the castle. I took a photo of it because I knew nobody would believe me when I got back. They still don't, even when I show them the photographic proof. But the photo is in front of me as I write, and a small stone from the castle, brought back as a memento, lies on the shelf to my right.

Regarding the flesh of Douglas, boiled from the bones, Barbour states:

The flesh with reverence profound
Was buried there in Holy ground.

Perhaps it was buried in Teba itself.

Back at the airport, awaiting the Glasgow flight, a few Scots asked me why I was in Spain. When I told them of the monument to Douglas and Robert the Bruce in Teba, several of them mentioned that they would have liked to have seen it. So, if you are holidaying on the Costa del Sol, go to Teba, have a beer and some chorizo in the Doblon De Oro (The Gold Doubloon) before visiting the monument at the top of the street, then look out over the battle-site from the castle. I can thoroughly recommend it.

Within a week of this trip, was in the Church of St Bride in Douglas, looking down at the effigy of Douglas himself, telling him how I had been to the battlesite at Teba. The heart said to be Douglas's can be seen under glass in the floor next to the step up to the altar; it sits in a leaden case.

Church of St Bride, Douglas

Douglas's tomb is very much defaced, and it is reported that it was vandalised by a detachment of Cromwell's troops, who, during their invasion of Scotland, used the church as a stable for their horses.

In the 1800s the Rev W Smith wrote:

Last century the school stood in the churchyard. There was no door on the choir, and the boys had full liberty to do as they liked, which liberty they undoubtedly took. So that the mutilation of statues attributed to Cromwell was performed by inferior destructionists. I may mention that, though the body of the Good Sir James was brought to Douglas according to tradition or history, no bones were found when recently the space under the stone effigy was opened.

Isn't that the saddest thing?

There are vaults beneath the church though, and perhaps Douglas's bones were interred somewhere below his tomb. Certainly they were returned to Douglas, as this is mentioned in several European chronicles. One worrying aspect is that when there was an enlargement and renovation of these vaults in 1879-

81, many old coffins were removed, and I am not aware of their fate after this time. I would hate to think the worst.

The vaults under the church were opened in the mid-1990s, and I found out about a week after the fact – something I have kicked myself for ever since. I am told that there is quite a sizeable structure below ground in good condition. The vaults are only opened periodically in order to be checked. Perhaps I shall be lucky next time. All that really remains intact of St Bride's today is the nave and a few other ruined portions surrounding it in the churchyard.

Tomb of the
Black Douglas

The clock in the little spire is said to be the oldest extant in Scotland, gifted by Mary Queen of Scots, and it bears on its face the date 1565. It is not always in working order, but when it is, it is kept a few minutes fast. The reason for this is because of the motto of the Douglases, stemming from the time of Bruce – 'Jamais Arriäre' – Never Behind. So their clock has to be ahead of everybody else's. Isn't that just the best?

The Douglas coat of arms changed at this time, to commemorate the carrying of the Bruce's heart. It had always been a white shield with a blue chief containing three white stars. After 1330, the shield was filled with a blood red heart in remembrance of Douglas's last commission.

Bruce's heart was returned to Melrose Abbey as he wished, and it lay buried there, in a known but unmarked site till later years. It was dug up in the mid 1990s, and the casket containing it was inserted into a new canister. This was re-buried in the Abbey grounds under a circular stone bearing the legend 'A noble heart may have no ease if freedom fail'. I was at the ceremony, and made a point of asking Historic Scotland's officials about its reburial. There is a concrete case set well underground, and the canister, bearing the same design as the stone above, is securely contained within it. It sits directly under the stone, and I mention this because I have heard rumours that the heart is elsewhere within the Abbey grounds. (MAP B11)

Plaque marking Bruce's heart

An interesting point I would like to raise is one regarding the plaque to Bruce in St Andrew's Church in Jerusalem. The plaque has a lion rampant shield surmounted by a crown, and below it states, 'In remembrance of the pious wish of King Robert Bruce that his heart should be buried in Jerusalem'. I am very pleased that such a plaque exists, but it was never Bruce's wish to have his

Bruce plaque, St Andrew's Church, Jerusalem

heart buried in Jerusalem, only presented there, before its return to Scotland. This plaque also has around its edge the following: 'In celebration of the sixth centenary of his death 1329 – 7th June – 1929 given by the citizens of Dunfermline and Melrose'.

It would seem sensible at this point to give Barbour's description of Douglas. He compiled this from information given to him by people who had known Douglas personally, a generation earlier.

But he was not so fair that we
Should speak greatly of his beauty.
In visage he was somewhat grey
And had black hair as I heard say.
But of limbs he was well made.
With bones great and shoulders broad
His body was well made and lengthy
As those that saw him said to me.
When he was blithe he was lovely
And meek and sweet in company
But when in battle might him see
All other countenance had he
And in speech he lisped somewhat
But that sat him right wonderous well.

On Bruce's death, Thomas Randolph assumed the title of Regent of Scotland, to rule while Bruce's son, David II, was a minor. He was Regent for only three years before English aggression once more began to cast its ugly shadow.

Randolph raised an army to counter the threat of invasion, and was at the head of this army at Cockburnspath in East Lothian when news came of an English invasion fleet entering the Forth. He turned back in an attempt to thwart their landing. Randolph had been suffering from gallstones, and his condition deteriorated when he reached Musselburgh. As he lay grievously ill, the inhabitants of the town formed a guard around the house in which he lay – such was the love that the people bore for the last surviving captain of Bannockburn. The townsfolk remained till word reached them that Randolph had died. For this loyal act Musselburgh has since been known as 'the honest town'. (MAP A17)

The house in which Randolph died stood until 1809. It was at the east end of the south side of the High Street. Randolph breathed his last on 20 July 1332, and like his uncle, the Bruce, he was interred with ceremony within Dunfermline Abbey, but unfortunately, no record exists of where he lies. Perhaps he is buried under the slabs that supposedly mark the tombs of the kings.

Chroniclers of the day were adamant that Randolph had been administered poison – an English plot – but this was probably propaganda.

Shield of Randolph

Barbour's description of Randolph says that he was of middle stature and compactly built. He had a pleasant open countenance and gentle manners. Certainly, as far as his skills as a fighting man and politician are concerned, there is no doubt that his death left a huge void that few could fill.

English aggression fills so much of our history books, and Scotland being much the smaller country, not only in terms of size, but of manpower and wealth too, the Scots have more often than not come out of each encounter worse off.

But it is not only the English who are to blame for Scotland's sometimes sorry state. All through Scotland's story I have read of those who took the side of the English, usually for wealth or land or simply for some perverted kind of Anglo-envy. For just a wee while though, Scotland showed what it was capable of when it stood as an entity. We at least had Bannockburn, but Scots seemed to forget quickly the lessons that Bruce strived so hard to instil in them. We can always take strength from the past, however, as we look to the future.

For that, Robert Bruce, I salute you.

Shield of Robert Bruce, King of Scots

Bibliography

Atlas of Scottish History to 1707
(University of Edinburgh, 1996)

Ordnance Gazetteer of Scotland
(William MacKenzie, London, 1893)

The Topographical, Statistical and Historical
Gazetteer of Scotland
(A. Fullarton & Co., Glasgow, 1842)

BARBOUR, John   The Bruce,
Edited by A.A.H. Douglas
(William MacLennan, Glasgow 1964)

BARRON, Evan   The Scottish War of Independence
First Published in 1914.
(Barnes & Noble, New York, 1997)

BARROW, G.W.S.   Robert Bruce
(Edinburgh University Press, Third Edition,
Edinburgh, 1988)

BOWER, Walter   Scotichronicon,
Edited by D.E.R. Watt
(Aberdeen University Press, 1991)

DALYELL, John
Graham   Monastic Antiquities
(George Ramsay & Co., Edinburgh, 1809)

DAVIS, I.M.   The Black Douglas
(Routledge and Kegan Paul, London, 1974)

FORDUN, John   Chronicle of the Scottish Nation
Edited by W.F. Skene
(Edmonston and Douglas, Edinburgh 1872)

HOWELL, Rev. A.R.   Paisley Abbey
                          (Alexander Gardner Ltd., Paisley, 1929)

JARDINE, Henry   Extracts from the report relative to the
(His Majesty's   tomb of King Robert Bruce 1821
Remembrancer)

MAXWELL, Herbert   Robert the Bruce
                          (G.P. Putnam's Sons, London, 1903)

MACKENZIE, Agnes   Robert Bruce
Mure   (A. Maclehose, London, 1934)

MCNAMEE, Colm   The Wars of Bruces
                          (Tuckwell Press, East Lothian, 1997)

PRESTWICH, Michael   Edward I
                          (Yale English Monarchs, Methven,
                          London, 1997)

SALTER, Mike   The Castles of Scotland Series, Five Volumes
                          (Folly Publications, Worcester, 1994)

SCOTT, Ronald   Robert the Bruce
McNair   (Canongate, Edinburgh, 1988)

TRANTER, Nigel   The Fortified House in Scotland,
                          Five Volumes
                          (The Mercat Press, Edinburgh, 1986)

WEBSTER, Rev. J.M.   Dunfermline Abbey
                          (The Carnegie Dunfermline Trust,
                          Dunfermline, 1948)

Some other books published by **LUATH** PRESS

ON THE TRAIL OF

On the Trail of William Wallace

David R. Ross

ISBN 0 946487 47 2 PBK £7.99

How close to reality was *Braveheart*?

Where was Wallace actually born?

What was the relationship between Wallace and Bruce?

Are there any surviving eye-witness accounts of Wallace?

How does Wallace influence the psyche of today's Scots?

On the Trail of William Wallace offers a refreshing insight into the life and heritage of the great Scots hero whose proud story is at the very heart of what it means to be Scottish. Not concentrating simply on the hard historical facts of Wallace's life, the book also takes into account the real significance of Wallace and his effect on the ordinary Scot through the ages, manifested in the many sites where his memory is marked.

In trying to piece together the jigsaw of the reality of Wallace's life, David Ross weaves a subtle flow of new information with his own observations. His engaging, thoughtful and at times amusing narrative reads with the ease of a historical novel, complete with all the intrigue, treachery and romance required to hold the attention of the casual reader and still entice the more knowledgable historian.

74 places to visit in Scotland and the north of England

One general map and 3 location maps

Stirling and Falkirk battle plans

Wallace's route through London

Chapter on Wallace connections in North America and elsewhere

Reproductions of rarely seen illustrations

On the Trail of William Wallace will be enjoyed by anyone with an interest in Scotland, from the passing tourist to the most fervent nationalist. It is an encyclopaedia-cum-guide book, literally stuffed with fascinating titbits not usually on offer in the conventional history book.

David Ross is organiser of and historical adviser to the Society of William Wallace.

'*Historians seem to think all there is to be known about Wallace has already been uncovered. Mr Ross has proved that Wallace studies are in fact in their infancy.*' ELSPETH KING, Director the the Stirling Smith Art Museum & Gallery, who annotated and introduced the recent Luath edition of *Blind Harry's Wallace*.

'*Better the pen than the sword!*' RANDALL WALLACE, author of *Braveheart*, when asked by David Ross how it felt to be partly responsible for the freedom of a nation following the Devolution Referendum.

On the Trail of Mary Queen of Scots

J. Keith Cheetham

ISBN 0 946487 50 2 PBK £7.99

Life dealt Mary Queen of Scots love, intrigue, betrayal and tragedy in generous measure.

On the Trail of Mary Queen of Scots traces the major events in the turbulent life of the beautiful, enigmatic queen whose romantic reign and tragic destiny exerts an undimmed fascination over 400 years after her execution.

Places of interest to visit – 99 in Scotland, 35 in England and 29 in France.

One general map and 6 location maps.

Line drawings and illustrations.

Simplified family tree of the royal houses of Tudor and Stuart.

Key sites include:

Linlithgow Palace - Mary's birthplace, now a magnificent ruin

Stirling Castle - where, only nine months old, Mary was crowned Queen of Scotland

Notre Dame Cathedral - where, aged fifteen, she married the future king of France

The Palace of Holyroodhouse - Rizzio, one of Mary's closest advisers, was murdered here and some say his blood still stains the spot where he was stabbed to death

Sheffield Castle - where for fourteen years she languished as prisoner of her cousin, Queen Elizabeth I

Fotheringhay - here Mary finally met her death on the executioner's block.

On the Trail of Mary Queen of Scots is for everyone interested in the life of perhaps the most romantic figure in Scotland's history; a thorough guide to places connected with Mary, it is also a guide to the complexities of her personal and public life.

'In my end is my beginning' MARY QUEEN OF SCOTS

'...the woman behaves like the Whore of Babylon' JOHN KNOX

On the Trail of Robert Service

GW Lockhart

ISBN 0 946487 24 3 PBK £7.99

Robert Service is famed worldwide for his eye-witness verse-pictures of the Klondike goldrush. As a war poet, his work out-sold Owen and Sassoon, and he went on to become the world's first million selling poet. In search of adventure and new experiences, he emigrated from Scotland to Canada in 1890 where he was caught up in the after-math of the raging gold fever. His vivid dramatic verse bring to life the wild, larger than life characters of the gold rush Yukon, their bar-room brawls, their lust for gold, their trigger-happy gambles with life and love. 'The Shooting of Dan McGrew' is perhaps his most famous poem:

A bunch of the boys were whooping it up
in the Malamute saloon;
The kid that handles the music box was
hitting a ragtime tune;
Back of the bar in a solo game, sat
Dangerous Dan McGrew,
And watching his luck was his light
o'love, the lady that's known as Lou.

His storytelling powers have brought Robert Service enduring fame, particularly in North America and Scotland where he is something of a cult figure.

Starting in Scotland, *On the Trail of Robert Service* follows Service as he wanders through British Columbia, Oregon, California, Mexico, Cuba, Tahiti, Russia, Turkey and the Balkans, finally 'settling' in France.

This revised edition includes an expanded selection of illustrations of scenes from the Klondike as well as several photographs from the family of Robert Service on his travels around the world.

Wallace Lockhart, an expert on Scottish traditional folk music and dance, is the author of *Highland Balls & Village Halls* and *Fiddles & Folk*. His relish for a well-told tale

in popular vernacular led him to fall in love with the verse of Robert Service and write his biography.

'A fitting tribute to a remarkable man - a bank clerk who wanted to become a cowboy. It is hard to imagine a bank clerk writing such lines as:

A bunch of boys were whooping it up...
The income from his writing actually exceeded his bank salary by a factor of five and he resigned to pursue a full time writing career.' Charles Munn, THE SCOTTISH BANKER

'Robert Service claimed he wrote for those who wouldnit be seen dead reading poetry. His was an almost unbelievably mobile life... Lockhart hangs on breathlessly, enthusiastically unearthing clues to the poet's life.' Ruth Thomas, SCOTTISH BOOK COLLECTOR

'This enthralling biography will delight Service lovers in both the Old World and the New.' Marilyn Wright, SCOTS INDEPEN-DENT

Blind Harry's Wallace

William Hamilton of Gilbertfield

ISBN 0 946487 43 X HBK £15.00
ISBN 0 946487 33 2 PBK £8.99

The original story of the real braveheart, Sir William Wallace. Racy, blood on every page, violently anglo-phobic, grossly embell-ished, vulgar and disgust-ing, clumsy and stilted, a literary failure, a great epic.

Whatever the verdict on BLIND HARRY, this is the book which has done more than any other to frame the notion of Scotland's national identity. Despite its numerous 'historical inaccuracies', it remains the principal source for what we now know about the life of Wallace.

The novel and film *Braveheart* were based on the 1722 Hamilton edition of this epic poem. Burns, Wordsworth, Byron and others were greatly influenced by this version 'wherein the old obsolete words are rendered more intelli-gible', which is said to be the book, next to the Bible, most commonly found in Scottish households in the eighteenth century. Burns even admits to having 'borrowed... a couplet worthy of Homer' directly from Hamilton's version of BLIND HARRY to include in *Scots wha hae*.

Elspeth King, in her introduction to this, the

first accessible edition of BLIND HARRY in verse form since 1859, draws parallels between the situation in Scotland at the time of Wallace and that in Bosnia and Chechnya in the 1990s. Seven hundred years to the day after the Battle of Stirling Bridge, the 'Settled Will of the Scottish People' was expressed in the devolution referendum of 11 September 1997. She describes this as a landmark opportunity for mature reflection on how the nation has been shaped, and sees BLIND HARRY'S WALLACE as an essential and compelling text for this purpose.

'Builder of the literary foundations of a national hero-cult in a free and powerful country'.

ALEXANDER STODDART, sculptor

'A true bard of the people'

TOM SCOTT, THE PENGUIN BOOK OF SCOTTISH VERSE, on Blind Harry.

'A more inventive writer than Shakespeare'

RANDALL WALLACE

'The story of Wallace poured a Scottish prejudice in my veins which will boil along until the floodgates of life shut in eternal rest'.

ROBERT BURNS

'Hamilton's couplets are not the best poetry you will ever read, but they rattle along at a fair pace. In re-issuing this work, the publishers have re-opened the spring from which most of our conceptions of the Wallace legend come'.

SCOTLAND ON SUNDAY

'The return of Blind Harry's Wallace, a man who makes Mel look like a wimp'.

THE SCOTSMAN

The Bannockburn Years

William Scott
ISBN 0 946487 34 0 PBK £7.95

A present day Edinburgh solicitor stumbles across reference to a document of value to the Nation State of Scotland. He tracks down the document on the Isle of Bute, a document which probes the real 'quaestiones' about nationhood and national identity. The document ends up being published, but is it authentic and does it matter? Almost 700 years on, these 'quaestiones' are still worth asking. Written with pace and passion, William Scott has devised an intriguing vehicle to open up new ways of looking at the future of Scotland and its people. He presents an alternative interpretation of how the Battle of Bannockburn was fought,

and through the Bannatyne manuscript he draws the reader into the minds of those involved.

Winner of the 1997 Constable Trophy, the premier award in Scotland for an unpublished novel, this book offers new insights to both the academic and the general reader which are sure to provoke further discussion and debate.

'A brilliant storyteller. I shall expect to see your name writ large hereafter.'
NIGEL TRANTER, October 1997

'... a compulsive read.' PH SCOTT, *The Scotsman*

Notes from the North
incorporating a Brief History of the Scots and the English

Emma Wood
ISBN 0 946487 46 4 PBK £8.99

Notes on being English
Notes on being in Scotland
Learning from a shared past

Is it time to recognise that the border between Scotland and England is the dividing line between very different cultures?

As the Scottish nation begins to set its own agenda, will it decide to consign its sense of grievance against England to the dustbin of history?

Will a fresh approach heal these ancient 'sibling rivalries'?

How does a study of Scottish history help to clarify the roots of Scottish-English antagonism?

Does an English 'white settler' have a right to contribute to the debate?

Will the empowering of the citizens of Scotland take us all, Scots and English, towards mutual tolerance and understanding?

Sickened by the English jingoism that surfaced in rampant form during the 1982 Falklands War, Emma Wood started to dream of moving from her home in East Anglia to the Highlands of Scotland. She felt increasingly frustrated and marginalised as Thatcherism got a grip on the southern English psyche. The Scots she met on frequent holidays in the Highlands had no truck with Thatcherism, and she felt at home with grass-roots Scottish anti-authoritarianism. The decision was made. She uprooted and headed for a new life in the north of Scotland.

She was to discover that she had crossed a border in more than the geographical sense.

Loving her new life and friends in first Sutherland and then Ross-shire, she nevertheless had to come to terms with the realisation that in the eyes of some Scots she was an unwelcome 'white settler' who would never belong. She became aware of the perception that some English incomers were insensitive to the needs and aspirations of Highland communities.

Her own approach has been thoughtful and creative. In *Notes from the North* she sets a study of Scots-English conflicts alongside relevant personal experiences of contemporary incomers' lives in the Highlands. She gently and perceptively confronts the issue of racial intolerance, and sets out conflicting perceptions of 'Englishness' and 'Scottishness'; she argues that racial stereotyping is a stultifying cul-de-sac, and that distinctive ethnic and cultural strands within Scottish society are potentially enriching and strengthening forces. This book is a pragmatic, positive and forward-looking contribution to cultural and politicial debate within Scotland.

Notes from the North is essential reading for anyone who is thinking of moving to Scotland and for Scots who want to move into the 21st century free of unnecessary baggage from the past.

Old Scotland New Scotland

Jeff Fallow

ISBN 0 946487 40 5   PBK   £6.99

'Together we can build a new Scotland based on Labour's values.' DONALD DEWAR, Party Political Broadcast

'Despite the efforts of decent Mr Dewar, the voters may yet conclude they are looking at the same old hacks in brand new suits.' IAN BELL, *The Independent*

'At times like this you suddenly realise how dangerous the neglect of Scottish history in our schools and universities may turn out to be.' MICHAEL FRY, *The Herald*

'...one of the things I hope will go is our chip on the shoulder about the English... The SNP has a huge responsibility to articulate Scottish independence in a way that is pro-Scottish and not anti-English.' ALEX SALMOND, *The Scotsman*

Scottish politics have never been more exciting. In *old Scotland new Scotland* Jeff Fallow takes us on a graphic voyage through Scotland's turbulent histo-

ry, from earliest times through to the present day and beyond. This fast-track guide is the quick way to learn what your history teacher didn't tell you, essential reading for all who seek an understanding of Scotland and its history.

Eschewing the romanticisation of his country's past, Fallow offers a new perspective on an old nation. 'Too many people associate Scottish history with tartan trivia or outworn romantic myth. This book aims to blast that stubborn idea.' JEFF FALLOW

Scotland, Land and People: An Inhabited Solitude

James McCarthy

ISBN 0 946487 57 X PBK £7.99

'Scotland is the country above all others that I have seen, in which a man of imagination may carve out his own pleasures; there are so many inhabited solitudes.' DOROTHY WORDSWORTH, in her journal of August 1803

An informed and thought-provoking profile of Scotland's unique landscapes and the impact of humans on what we see now and in the future. James McCarthy leads us through the many aspects of the land and the people who inhabit it: natural Scotland; the rocks beneath; land ownership; the use of resources; people and place; conserving Scotland's heritage and much more.

Written in a highly readable style, this concise volume offers an understanding of the land as a whole. Emphasising the uniqueness of the Scottish environment, the author explores the links between this and other aspects of our culture as a key element in rediscovering a modern sense of the Scottish identity and perception of nationhood. 'This book provides an engaging introduction to the mysteries of Scotland's people and landscapes. Difficult concepts are described in simple terms, providing the interested Scot or tourist with an invaluable overview of the country... It fills an important niche which, to my knowledge, is filled by no other publications.' BETSY KING, Chief Executive, Scottish Environmental Education Council.

Over the Top with the Tartan Army (Active Service 1992-97)

Andrew McArthur

ISBN 0 946487 45 6 PBK £7.99

Scotland has witnessed the growth of a new

and curious military phenomenon – grown men bedecked in tartan yomping across the globe, hellbent on benevolence and ritualistic bevvying. What noble cause does this famous army serve? Why, football of course!

Taking us on an erratic world tour, McArthur gives a frighteningly funny insider's eye view of active service with the Tartan Army – the madcap antics of Scotland's travelling support in the '90s, written from the inside, covering campaigns and skirmishes from Euro '92 up to the qualifying drama for France '98 in places as diverse as Russia, the Faroes, Belarus, Sweden, Monte Carlo, Estonia, Latvia, USA and Finland.

This book is a must for any football fan who likes a good laugh.

'I commend this book to all football supporters'.
GRAHAM SPIERS, *Scotland on Sunday*

'In wishing Andy McArthur all the best with this publication, I do hope he will be in a position to produce a sequel after our participation in the World Cup in France'. CRAIG BROWN, Scotland Team Coach

All royalties on sales of the book are going to Scottish charities, principally Children's Hospice Association Scotland, the only Scotland-wide charity of its kind, providing special love and care to children with terminal illnesses at its hospice, Rachel House, in Kinross.

A Word for Scotland

Jack Campbell
with a foreword by Magnus Magnusson
ISBN 0 946487 48 0 PBK £12.99

The inside story of a newspaper and a nation – five tumultuous decades as they happened.

'A word for Scotland' was Lord Beaver-brook's hope when he founded the *Scottish Daily Express*. That word for Scotland quickly became, and was for many years, the national newspaper of Scotland.

The pages of *A Word For Scotland* exude warmth and a wry sense of humour. Jack Campbell takes us behind the scenes to meet the larger-than-life characters and ordinary people who made and recorded the stories. Here we hear the stories behind the stories that hit the headlines in this great yarn of journalism in action.

Jack joined the infant newspaper at the age of 15 as a copy-boy. The young lad from Govan went on to become a leading player through nearly half a century of the most exciting, innovative and competitive years of the press in Scotland, finishing up as managing editor. He remembers the early days of news-gathering on a shoestring, the circulation wars, all the scoops and dramas and tragedies through nearly half a century of the most exciting, innovative and competitive years of the press in Scotland. He was with the *Scottish Daily Express* through the dramatic events of 1974 which ended the paper's long reign at 195 Albion Street, Glasgow.

It would be true to say 'all life is here'. From the Cheapside Street fire of which cost the lives of 19 Glasgow firemen, to the theft of the Stone of Destiny, to the lurid exploits of serial killer Peter Manuel, to encounters with world boxing champions Benny Lynch and Cassius Clay – this book offers telling glimpses of the characters, events, joy and tragedy which make up Scotland's story in the 20th century.

'As a rookie reporter you were proud to work on it and proud to be part of it - it was fine newspaper right at the heartbeat of Scotland.'
RONALD NEIL, Chief Executive of BBC Production, and a reporter on the *Scottish Daily Express* (1963-68)

'This book is a fascinating reminder of Scottish journalism in its heyday. It will be read avidly by those journalists who take pride in their profession – and should be compulsory reading for those who don't.'
JACK WEBSTER, columnist on *The Herald* and *Scottish Daily Express* journalist (1960-80)

LUATH GUIDES TO SCOTLAND

Highways and Byways in Mull and Iona
Peter Macnab
ISBN 0 946487 16 2 PBK £4.25

Southwest Scotland
Tom Atkinson
ISBN 0 946487 04 9 PBK £4.95

The Lonely Lands
Tom Atkinson
ISBN 0 946487 10 3 PBK £4.95

The Empty Lands
Tom Atkinson
ISBN 0 946487 13 8 PBK £4.95

Roads to the Isles
Tom Atkinson
ISBN 0 946487 01 4 PBK £4.95

NATURAL SCOTLAND

Wild Scotland: the essential guide to finding the best of natural Scotland
James McCarthy
Photography by Laurie Campbell
ISBN 0 946487 37 5 PBK £7.50

Rum: Nature's Island
Magnus Magnusson
ISBN 0 946487 32 4 PBK £7.95

The Highland Geology Trail
John L Roberts
ISBN 0 946487 36 7 PBK £4.99

FOLKLORE

Tall Tales from an Island
Peter Macnab
ISBN 0 946487 07 3 PBK £8.99

The Supernatural Highlands
Francis Thompson
ISBN 0 946487 31 6 PBK £8.99

WALK WITH LUATH

Mountain Days & Bothy Nights
Dave Brown and Ian Mitchell
ISBN 0 946487 15 4 PBK £7.50

The Joy of Hillwalking
Ralph Storer
ISBN 0 946487 28 6 PBK £7.50

Scotland's Mountains before the Mountaineers
Ian Mitchell
ISBN 0 946487 39 1 PBK £9.99

LUATH WALKING GUIDES

Walks in the Cairngorms
Ernest Cross
ISBN 0 946487 09 X PBK £3.95

Short Walks in the Cairngorms
Ernest Cross
ISBN 0 946487 23 5 PBK £3.95

SPORT

Ski & Snowboard Scotland
Hilary Parke
ISBN 0 946487 35 9 PBK £6.99

SOCIAL HISTORY

The Crofting Years
Francis Thompson
ISBN 0 946487 06 5 PBK £6.95

MUSIC AND DANCE

Highland Balls and Village Halls
GW Lockhart
ISBN 0 946487 12 X PBK £6.95

Fiddles & Folk: a celebration of the re-emergence of Scotland's musical heritage
GW Lockhart
ISBN 0 946487 38 3 PBK £7.95

FICTION

The Great Melnikov
Hugh MacLachlan
ISBN 0 946487 42 1 PBK £7.95

BIOGRAPHY

Tobermory Teuchter: a first-hand account of life on Mull in the early years of the 20th century
Peter Macnab
ISBN 0 946487 41 3 PBK £7.99

Bare Feet and Tackety Boots
Archie Cameron
ISBN 0 946487 17 0 PBK £7.95

Come Dungeons Dark
John Taylor Caldwell
ISBN 0 946487 19 7 PBK £6.95

On the Trail of Robert Service
G Wallace Lockhart
ISBN 0 946487 24 3 PBK £7.99

POETRY

Poems to be read aloud
Collected and with an introduction by Tom Atkinson
ISBN 0 946487 00 6 PBK £5.00

COMING SOON...

On the Trail of Robert Burns
John Cairney
ISBN 0 946487 51 0 PBK £7.99

On the Trail of Rob Roy MacGregor
John Barrington
ISBN 0 946487 59 6 PBK £7.99

Luath Press Limited
committed to publishing well written books worth reading

LUATH PRESS takes its name from Robert Burns, whose little collie Luath (*Gael.*, swift or nimble) tripped up Jean Armour at a wedding and gave him the chance to speak to the woman who was to be his wife and the abiding love of his life. Burns called one of *The Twa Dogs* Luath after Cuchullin's hunting dog in *Ossian's Fingal*. Luath Press grew up in the heart of Burns country, and now resides a few steps up the road from Burns' first lodgings in Edinburgh's Royal Mile.

Luath offers you distinctive writing with a hint of unexpected pleasures.

Most UK bookshops either carry our books in stock or can order them for you. To order direct from us, please send a £sterling cheque, postal order, international money order or your credit card details (number, address of cardholder and expiry date) to us at the address below. Please add post and packing as follows: UK – £1.00 per delivery address; overseas surface mail – £2.50 per delivery address; overseas airmail – £3.50 for the first book to each delivery address, plus £1.00 for each additional book by airmail to the same address. If your order is a gift, we will happily enclose your card or message at no extra charge.

Luath Press Limited
543/2 Castlehill
The Royal Mile
Edinburgh EH1 2ND
Telephone: 0131 225 4326 (24 hours)
Fax: 0131 225 4324
email: gavin.macdougall@luath.co.uk
Website: www.luath.co.uk